WILD ALBERTA AT THE CROSSROADS

Wild Alberta

AT THE CROSSROADS

a personal journey by MARIAN WHITE and ROBIN WHITE

photography by ROBIN WHITE

foreword by Andrew Nikiforuk

NATUREWATCH PRESS

Published in Canada by NatureWatch Press,
 a division of NatureWatch Ltd.
Box 74048, Strathcona RPO
Calgary, Alberta, Canada T3H 3B6
403 246-2994
marian.nw@nucleus.com
www.naturewatchworld.com

Cover and book design by Frances Hunter
Editing by Joyce Hildebrand, Alberta Wilderness
 Association, Calgary, AB
Cartography by Robin Poitras, Calgary, AB
Printed and bound in China by Everbest

HC 07 08 09 10 11   5 4 3 2 1

Library and Archives Canada Cataloguing in Publication
White, Marian, 1943–
    Wild Alberta at the crossroads : a personal journey /
by Marian White and Robin White ; photography by Robin White ;
foreword by Andrew Nikiforuk.

Includes bibliographical references and index.
ISBN 978-0-9783849-0-6

    1. Natural history—Alberta. 2. Natural history—Alberta—
Pictorial works. 3. Nature conservation—Alberta. 4. Nature
conservation—Alberta—Pictorial works. I. White, Robin, 1939–
II. Title.

QH106.2.A4W44 2007   508.7123   C2007-903949-9

PHOTOGRAPHER'S NOTES

Truth in photography: All animals and plants (including the puffball mushroom) were photographed in the wild except for the whooping crane (portrait only), wolf, and lynx, which are captive. As for Mr. Bogle, the great horned owl (who is named after a local politician), his portrait was taken at the Alberta Birds of Prey Centre in Coaldale, where he teaches ornithology 101.
    Equipment: All images were taken with Nikon cameras and lenses. Field notes were recorded in small notebooks using a variety of ball point pens.

PERMISSIONS AND SOURCES

The two Swan Hills aerial photos (pages 154-55) are AS 0120_125 and AS 4209_115, copyright © Government of Alberta under the *Copyright Act of Canada*; reproduced with permission from Air Photo Distribution, Alberta Sustainable Resource Development; tel 780 427-8148, www.srd.gov.ab.ca/land/g_airphotos.
    The law excerpt, pages 157-58, is reprinted from *Unnatural Law: Rethinking Canadian Environmental Law and Policy* by David R. Boyd © University of British Columbia Press 2003, with permission of the publisher. All rights reserved by the publisher; www.ubcpress.ca.
    The maps were based on the detailed Natural Regions and Subregions of Alberta map jointly published by Alberta Sustainable Resource Development, Alberta Environment, Alberta Community Development and Agriculture, and Agri-Food Canada, June 2005; toll free 877 944-0313.

SUPPORT RECEIVED

The publisher gratefully acknowledges the support, financially or in kind, received from the Alberta Wilderness Association and The Camera Store, both of Calgary, Alberta; and LightHawk of Lander, Wyoming, a nonprofit environmental aviation organization.

FRONTISPIECE: *Native grasses and sage sweep south to the Sweetgrass Hills along the border with Montana.*

To the wild animals and native plants
of Alberta, which cannot speak for themselves, and
to all who speak and act on their behalf.

Contents

FACING PAGE: *The great-horned owl is a most impressive and versatile bird, nesting in all natural regions of Alberta. It is the official bird of this province.*

FOREWORD
by Andrew Nikiforuk

My family and I moved to Alberta in 1991 and it was a revelation. We found blue skies, snowcapped mountains, and open spaces. Even the neighbours talked to each other. The bluebirds sang and the streets of Calgary were rich with civic imaginations. And so I learned, as the great American writer Wallace Stegner discovered, that "the West is hope's native home." He even called it "the geography of hope." Anyone who has ever paddled Lake Waterton or hiked the cold Peyto Glacier knows this profound truth.

But Alberta has since boomed and every day this exaggerated and greedy hurricane destroys another river, forest, or rural community. The province has carelessly accepted the undebated premise that it's okay to sacrifice a quarter of its northern forests for tar sand development and other fossil fuel addictions. As a consequence, Alberta now boasts an Ontario-style incivility, traffic jams, contaminated groundwater, and one of the nation's worst crime and drug rates. The scale of grave robbing and scenery looting is unparalleled. Even the air tastes of avarice.

So I have learned that there are varieties and degrees of hope and that unrealistic expectations are fast foods that Alberta and the Canadian West have gobbled far too often.

Stegner, too, found a wise explanation for this sort of behaviour, in his own parents. One was a sticker and one was a boomer. Their sad western marriage aptly mirrors Alberta's predicament and explains why so many wild places are being ruined here.

Stegner's mother was an inveterate sticker or nester. The Iowa-born farm girl believed "in all the beauties and strengths and human associations of place." She thought life was about giving and not getting, and she understood the limits that aridity imposes on dry lands. But she married a charming boomer and professional vandal who refused to stay put or accept limits. To him the West was one big, unguarded candy store. Rivers existed to be polluted and grasslands were treasure boxes to be looted.

Stegner's dad felt that world didn't owe him a living but a killing. To that end he pillaged one place after another. First, he cut trees and then he upturned buffalo grass. He speculated for gold, ploughed up more native grass, ran a gambling joint, chopped down more trees, and finally died broke and friendless in a fleabag hotel, "having in his lifetime done more human and environmental damage than he could have repaired in a second lifetime." Stegner's dad and Ralph Klein, the careless architect of booming Alberta, would have been good drinking pals.

The crazy energy and self-deception that drove Stegner's father have now infected much of this province. Every week hundreds of new migrants swagger into Alberta with visions of getting rich on the proceeds of hydrocarbon. I doubt many will retire here. It's obvious that boomers outnumber stickers in the circles of power, too.

But the best and most beautiful part of Canada, as illustrated by this wonderful book, deserves a better ethic and Stegner's grace for place. True stickers can't remain silent during a carnival for boomers. The real work of province-making demands local affection, which is something a gambler can never provide. Sticking demands slowing down and settling in. It means buying food from local farmers and defending watersheds. It means conserving wild places because, unlike the ugly strip mines of the tar sands, they provide a Godly solace. It means walking more and driving less. Being a sticker requires a fidelity to the land: being present, competent, and self-sufficient in all things. Finally, it's about appreciating the beauty of wild Alberta and defending this place with a courageous heart.

I invite every reader of this book to now make a sticker's investment in Alberta by defending our geography of hope, our lands, air, and water, against further abuse. We stand at a dangerous crossroad where we can either think of our children's welfare or write them off as another endangered species of caribou. Without wilderness, there is no civilization. And without a civilized respect for wild places there is no real future worth imagining.

Such action should probably begin with one rude and fiercely moral question: are we here to make a living or to make a killing?

This book is a reminder that living well has nothing to do with murdering one hopeful place after another.

PREFACE

Turning Point   Marian White

AND NOW THEY WERE FALLING – five roped climbers yanked from their footholds on a steep mountain-face in the Canadian Rockies. The collapse of a cornice had triggered an avalanche that sent the men hurtling, airborne in a haze of snow and ice shards. Propelled clean over a gaping crevasse, they tumbled, then slithered until, at last, they came to rest on the steep snowfield below.

Slowly, they staggered to their feet. All, that is, except one: Jay lay still, his back broken. As the team scrambled to carry him to safety on a makeshift stretcher, adrenalin masked the pain in Robin's severely damaged knee. That fateful day

FACING PAGE: *While descending this ridge on Mount Robson, an avalanche swept Robin's climbing party down to the snowfield below. The injuries he sustained marked a turning point in our lives.*

on Mount Robson in July 1977 changed his life and mine forever.

I was elsewhere at the time, hiking back-country passes with the Cheerful Charlies hiking group, for, like Robin, mountains were my passion. My own love affair with wild landscapes had taken off during a weeklong high-school field trip to the mountains of the English Lake District soon after I turned 17. Back then Robin, a stranger still, was already climbing mountains in Wales and Switzerland, and four years later I began climbing there with friends, too. That's how Robin and I first met – waiting out a storm at a mountain hut high in the Swiss Alps. Our need for adventure and communion with large, wild places had finally brought us together.

Strangely, we share this passion with none of our relatives. And growing up in the suburbs of London, England, we experienced only the tiniest glowing embers of wild nature. Yet those were enough to spark a yearning for something other than the overpopulated, overbuilt, over-roaded land that gave us birth.

So, in our late twenties, we embarked in 1968 on the first of many journeys through the deserts, mountains, forests, and grasslands, and the towns and villages of the world. Those early travels, within some of the poorest countries, marked the first and most profound turning point in our lives. They opened our eyes to the natural beauty and diversity of the planet, forced us to re-examine our beliefs and values, and taught us what in life is important and what is not. One result was our not returning to England. In July 1970, with only $300 left in our pockets, we put our vagabond ways behind us and launched upon a new life in a new land: Canada.

Our travels had generated more questions than answers and this soon led to university studies in Toronto. We emerged more knowledgeable not just about Nature and the natural systems upon which all life depends, but about the need to address the growing human footprint. Then, yearning again for mountains and the solitude of wilderness, we headed in 1975 to Alberta – our home ever since.

JAY'S BROKEN BACK HEALED SURPRISINGLY FAST. But the extensive damage to the cartilage and ligaments of Robin's left knee left him questioning whether he would ever walk properly again, let alone run, climb, or ski. Until the accident, our lust for hard physical exercise had shaped our weekend agendas of hiking and climbing, but we were forced, now, to adopt a slower pace. Far from restricting us, however, this opened our eyes to another world: the lives of wild plants and animals. Rope and ice axes yielded to binoculars and camera; climbing guidebooks to flower and bird guides.

Photography had always been Robin's passion and now there was more time for it. We would spend hours lying on our bellies in alpine meadows waiting for the wind to drop so we could photograph wildflowers or sitting quietly in a blind as a ruffed grouse proudly drummed on a log three paces away. And something else happened. As our knowledge of wilderness and the natural world became more intimate, there arose a new feeling: a spiritual awakening, a transcendent sense of being a part of the Whole – of truly coming home at last.

TWENTY WORK-YEARS PASSED. It was time for reflection. After years as a technical editor in the oil patch, I had quit and started a small business providing stock photography, writing, and editing to industry and the educational field. Robin worked at the City of Calgary, leading a team of planners designing new suburban communities that supported public transit, walking, cycling, and reduced car dependency.

We'd continued travelling abroad on our annual holidays. But our focus was shifting from geographical and cultural landscapes toward biodiversity and conservation. On returning, through slide shows we'd share with audiences our

FACING PAGE: *Grizzly bear. While large predators went extinct in most of overpopulated Europe long ago, Alberta's continue to roam – for now.*

experience of the wildlife and peoples of far-off lands, and how environmental damage and the worsening human condition typically go hand in hand. And we tried to walk our talk, raising awareness and funds to help protect forests, alleviate poverty, and educate children in Africa, Madagascar, and Nepal. But what about our own home? What about Alberta?

We came from a land that has 20 times Alberta's population but only one-third its land base, where wildness hangs by a thread and brown bear and lynx, boar, wolf, and beaver are long gone. Today, Britain's wild bird populations have shrunk to half their 1970 numbers – even the ubiquitous house sparrows are vanishing and its pollinating butterflies and bumblebees are in steep decline or already going extinct. It's a recipe for disaster. Not surprisingly, Robin and I are in awe of Alberta's remaining wildness: the diversity of her natural landscapes and wildlife, from grizzly bear and curlews to orchids and bull trout.[1]

True, the massive wave of early settlement on the prairie and parkland degraded and fragmented those natural regions (see map, page 16), and energy-industry activities expanded the human footprint from 1949 onward. But some wild expanses and most wild species that were around 150 years ago – even large carnivores at the top of the food chain – somehow still survive here. It is these – our soils, forests, grasslands, wetlands, plants, and animals, superbly co-evolved with the climate – that are Alberta's real wealth, her natural capital. Collectively, they underpin Alberta's economy and the quality of life of her citizens.

BACK, NOW, TO OUR STORY. In 1998, Robin decided it was time to quit the City and do something different. While we had come to know Alberta's mountain parks and a few prairie locales well, we knew the land north of Edmonton not at all. Nor had we paddled her great rivers or driven an ice-road. It was time to go exploring again – this time, our homeland.

A routine evolved. We would rent out our house each May through October. Then, using *Song Dog*, our camper, as a mobile base, we spent seven years exploring wild places we'd never been before and old haunts we had come to love. Along the way we learned from ranchers, First Nations people, conservationists, biologists, and many others. Much of what we saw and heard was magical, but much of it was alarming. It was time to write a book.

Most coffee-table books about Nature celebrate it and so do we. The more you learn about it, the more fascinating Nature becomes, and we enjoy sharing our experiences and images with others. But today celebration is not enough. Our generation inherited the Earth from previous generations and we owe it to our children and grandchildren to be good stewards. We aren't – and most Albertans know it. From one end of this province to the other, this paradise is under siege from human overuse and, indeed, abuse.

Certainly we are all to blame to some degree. Most of us can, and should, live more lightly on the Earth. And we should have done a far better job of holding our governments to account. We trusted them to develop an ecologically sustainable economy, manage our resources in the broad public interest, effectively regulate industrial pollution, and act responsibly in the global effort to prevent dangerous climate change. Overwhelmingly, they failed and most of us were too preoccupied with our daily lives to respond.

Now, ALBERTA STANDS AT THE CROSSROADS. Are we going to continue with our collective head in the sand, ignoring the environmental damage we are causing, or are we going to rethink our relationship with Nature and demand that our leaders manage this province more responsibly?

Ours is intended as a transformative book. People won't fight for something they don't understand and have little attachment to. So we hope that the images, stories, and natural history in Part One, "Exploring Wild Alberta," will encourage you to pause in your busy life, buy some Nature guides and a pair of binoculars, and set about rediscovering wild Alberta for yourself.

At the same time, we want to raise people's awareness of some of the key conservation issues affecting each natural region, and we do this chapter by chapter. Part Two, "At the Crossroads," has three chapters: in "Losing Our Way," we try to put our finger on what must be done to address the systemic problems and get Alberta on track to a more sustainable future. In "Finding the Path" we address the question: "But what can someone like me do to make a difference?" Here you'll find examples of exciting initiatives by Albertans who aren't just wringing their hands and complaining, but are taking action, typically in concert with others, to forge a sustainable future. There's a whole raft of things that anyone can do to make a difference, and in "Getting Started, Striding Out" you'll find some handy resources and tips on how to begin re-establishing a connection with the natural world; how to get up to speed on the issues; and how to help protect wild Alberta – our life support system – for our children.

So this is our story. Nearly thirty years ago a close call on a mountainside triggered a turning point in our lives. We hope this book will spark a turning point in your own.

Natural Regions
and
Subregions
of
ALBERTA

0   50   100 km

Natural Regions and Subregions

Canadian Shield
- Kazan Uplands

Boreal Forest
- Central Mixedwood
- Dry Mixedwood
- Northern Mixedwood
- Peace-Athabasca Delta
- Boreal Subarctic
- Upper Boreal Highlands
- Lower Boreal Highlands
- Athabasca Plain

Foothills
- Lower Foothills
- Upper Foothills

Rocky Mountain
- Alpine
- Subalpine
- Montane

Parkland
- Foothills Parkland
- Peace River Parkland
- Central Parkland

Grassland
- Dry Mixedgrass
- Foothills Fescue
- Northern Fescue
- Mixedgrass

Bistcho Lake
Fort Smith
Fitzgerald
Zama Lake
Margaret Lake
Han River
Slave River
Fort Chipewyan
Lake Athabasca
High Level
Peace River
Lake Claire
Chinchaga River
Gardiner Lake
Namur Lake
Manning
Bison Lake
Peerless Lake
Graham Lake
Fort McMurray
Athabasca River
Gordon Lake
Cardinal Lake
Fairview
Peace River
Kimiwan Lake
Utikuma Lake
Muskwa Lake
Wabasca Lakes
Sandy Lake
Pelican Lake
Winefred Lake
Smoky River
Grande Prairie
Winagami Lake
Lesser Slave Lake
Slave Lake
Calling Lake
Lac la Biche
Cold Lake
Valleyview
Swan Hills
Athabasca
Athabasca River
Muriel Lake
Frog Lake
Grande Cache
Whitecourt
North Saskatchewan River
Hinton
Edson
Edmonton
Beaverhill Lake
Lloydminster
Drayton Valley
Millet
Camrose
Jasper
Pigeon Lake
Killam
Wainwright
Battle River
Nordegg
Rocky Mountain House
Red Deer
Coronation
Sundre
Banff
Drumheller
Calgary
Red Deer River
Longview
Bow River
South Sask. River
Oldman River
Medicine Hat
Lethbridge
Foremost
Pakowki Lake
Cardston
Milk River
Waterton

Location and Size

- *Latitude*: 49° to 60° North and longitude 110° to 120° West.
- *Area*: 662,587 square kilometres (km²); Canada's fourth-largest province.
- *Length north to south*: 1,223 km. Width varies from 293 to 660 km.
- *Highest point*: Mount Columbia in Jasper National Park: 3,747 metres above sea level.

Natural Regions and Wildlife

- *Natural regions*: Rocky Mountain, Foothills, Grassland, Parkland, Boreal Forest, and Canadian Shield, divided into 21 subregions (see map opposite).
- *Number of known native species*: about 95 mammals; almost 400 birds (nesters plus migrants); 8 reptiles, 10 amphibians, and 63 fish; about 1,580 vascular plants; and thousands of non-vascular plants (such as moss and lichen) and insects.
- *Wildlife emblems*: flower – wild (prickly) rose; tree – lodgepole pine; grass – rough fescue; bird – great horned owl; mammal – Rocky Mountain bighorn sheep; fish – bull trout; mushroom – red cap, also called northern roughstem.

Land Ownership and Control

- *Ownership*: Over 60 percent is Crown land (land held in trust for the public) administered by the Government of Alberta – mostly forestry reserve. About 11 percent is Crown land administered by the Government of Canada – directly, in the case of national parks and military bases, and indirectly, regarding Indian reserves. The remaining 29 percent is privately owned.
- As for *subsurface rights* (to all minerals below the top 30 centimetres of the ground), the Government of Alberta holds those rights in trust for the Alberta public and sells them.
- *Provincial parks*: Alberta administers over 500 parks, reserves, and recreation areas covering about 27,500 km²; but see page 77.

- *National parks*: Banff, Jasper, Waterton Lakes, Wood Buffalo, and Elk Island.
- *National Wildlife Areas and Migratory Bird Sanctuaries* - four of each: the Blue Quills (northeast of Edmonton), Meanook (near Athabasca), Spiers Lake (east edge of Rumsey Moraine), and Suffield wildlife areas; and the Inglewood (Calgary), Red Deer, Saskatoon Lake (Grande Prairie), and Richardson Lake (south of Lake Athabasca) bird sanctuaries.

Sites Awarded Special International Status

- UNESCO *World Heritage Sites*: Canadian Rocky Mountain Parks (includes Banff and Jasper); Waterton-Glacier International Peace Park (includes Waterton Lakes National Park); Wood Buffalo National Park; Dinosaur Provincial Park; and Head-Smashed-In Buffalo Jump.
- *Ramsar sites*: These are sites listed as Wetlands of International Importance under the *Convention on Wetlands,* an international intergovernmental treaty signed in Ramsar, Iran, in 1971. Alberta has four: the Peace-Athabasca Delta, the Whooping Crane Summer Range astride the Alberta-Northwest Territories border, and Hay-Zama Lakes (all boreal); and Beaverhill Lake (parkland).
- *Important Bird Areas*: Alberta has 48. This program was founded in Europe in 1985 by BirdLife International, a non-governmental, umbrella bird conservation organization that is now global. The sites listed are highly significant and provide essential habitat for birds, including threatened and endemic species and birds in exceptional concentrations.

People and the Economy

- *Population*: 3.3 million (July 2006).
- *Major industries*: oil and gas, forestry, coal mining, agriculture, tourism, and gambling.

PART ONE

Exploring Wild Alberta

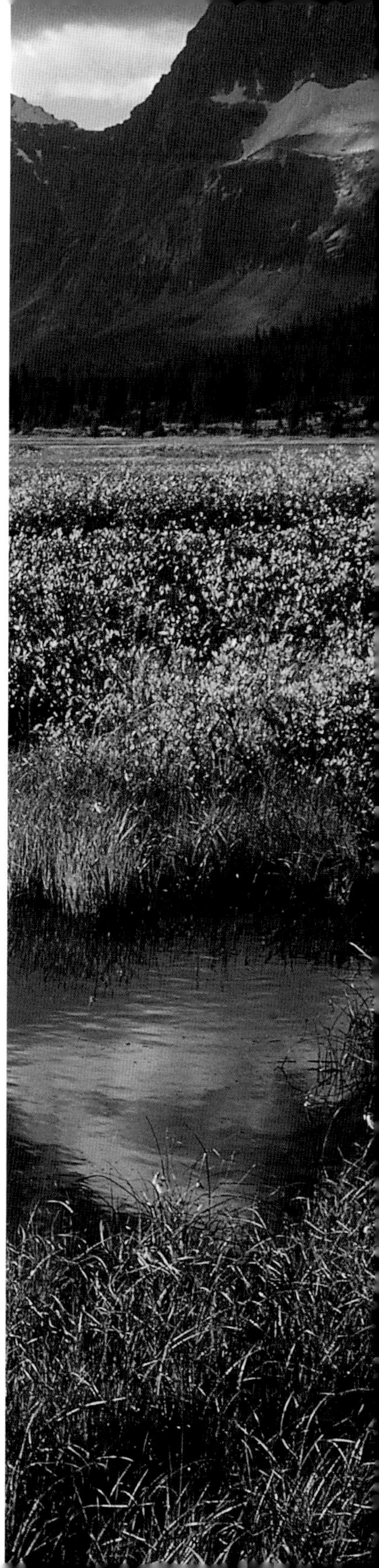

"Everybody needs ... places ...
where Nature may heal and cheer and
give strength to body and soul."

JOHN MUIR (1838–1914), FOUNDER OF THE SIERRA CLUB

THE MOUNTAINS

Life on the Rocks

Marian White

"THIS IS PARADISE," Kurt says, leaning back in his saddle. "We have nothing like this left in Germany." It is a perfect summer's day in the Tonquin Valley, Jasper National Park. We've been out all morning scouting for wildlife and are now resting on a prow of rock overlooking an alpine meadow lush with wildflowers. Kurt and his guided party of trailriders have ridden over to our viewpoint and stopped for lunch.

I follow Kurt's gaze west across the valley to the Ramparts towering above Amethyst Lake. He is right, of course. The Canadian Rockies are magnificent, one of the great mountain chains of the world. Their folded limestone front ranges rise tilting, knife-edged – a sudden, startling wall bounding the Great Plains. Westward, the square-shouldered dolomite and limestone main ranges crown the continental divide like the battlements of giants' fortresses. Here, icefields and glaciers feed lakes of astonishing turquoise, and waterfalls tumble fast and cold down the mountainsides.

"This morning," Kurt says, "we saw a bald eagle steal a fish from an osprey above Amethyst Lake." Olga, his wife, nods enthusiastically.

FACING PAGE: *Looking toward Eremite Valley and glacier from Tonquin Valley, Jasper National Park.*

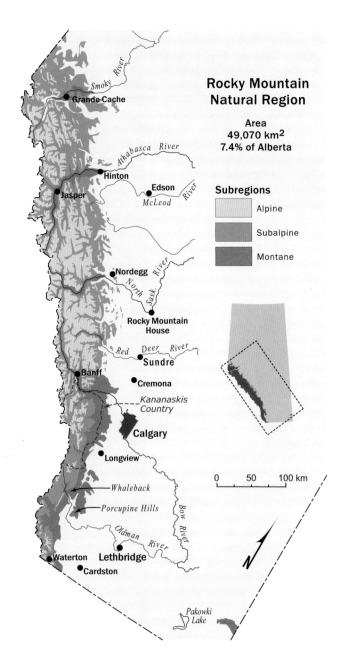

Rocky Mountain Natural Region

Area
49,070 km²
7.4% of Alberta

Subregions

Alpine

Subalpine

Montane

0   50   100 km

"And yesterday," she adds, "we saw a moose standing in Chrome Lake, feeding. And last night, two caribou walked past our cabin."

The others chip in with accounts of what they've seen. The guide had pointed out two grizzly bears high on Maccarib Pass. Several riders had seen a pair of porcupines eating their way through flowers in an alpine meadow like synchronized lawn mowers. One young fellow describes how, down at the boat dock, he'd watched a mother weasel carrying her babies one by one to a new burrow among the rocks. And the party has been in the valley only two days!

Kurt and Olga are here not simply for the scenic grandeur, since impressive mountain ranges exist on many continents. Nor are they here just to see large mammals. They can do that by visiting a zoo or renting a nature video. But to actually see grizzlies, caribou, and a full array of wildlife in the wild, living much as they have for millennia – that is what makes the Rockies so special.

As for us, it is our fifth Tonquin trip in four years to find and photograph the endangered mountain caribou. Many hikers serendipitously catch sight of them on their first visit and think nothing of it. But our dedicated efforts have mostly ended in frustration. Once, a trio of female caribou appeared only six paces from our campground table as we ate breakfast. By the time we had grabbed our camera gear from the tent, they were gone.

Now, I spy two magnificent bulls across the lake, dozing in a meadow. We hike there quickly through forest, then emerge slowly, eyes downcast to signal we are no threat. The caribou remain unperturbed. Fifty paces from them, Robin kneels behind his tripod, taking photographs, while I stand with my back to him, scanning with the scope for other wildlife. Time passes....

FACING PAGE: *Trailriders descend toward Amethyst Lake beneath the great cliffs of the Ramparts in Tonquin Valley, Jasper National Park.*

ALBERTA'S CARIBOU:
GREY GHOSTS OF THE FOREST

Alberta's caribou are woodland caribou. They form 18 herds (hunters exterminated the Swan Hills herd in the mid-1960s), divided between two distinct lifestyles. Thirteen boreal herds (85 percent of the caribou) stay year-round in the boreal forest. The five southern mountain herds inhabit alpine and subalpine meadows north of Banff in summer, and traditionally descended to foothills forest in winter.

The species is legally designated as threatened Canada-wide and in Alberta. The reasons? For one, it relies for food on lichen found only in old-growth forest, which is now fragmented and rapidly being cut down. For another, disturbance: studies have shown that caribou avoid forest within one kilometre of a road, whether in the mountains, the foothills, or the vast boreal forest. Three Alberta herds – Slave Lake (under 100 animals), North Banff (2 animals), and Little Smoky (50 animals) – face imminent extirpation, meaning they're doomed. Twelve more, including the 100-animal South Jasper herd (Tonquin/Maligne), are declining, some rapidly. Only three herds are stable. Because Alberta's caribou live mostly within remote northern forest, exact numbers are unknown. Perhaps more than 8,000 a century ago, they are thought to number only 3,000 or so today.

Despite 30 years of studies and talk, the Alberta government and industry have failed to recover the caribou herds or even stop their decline (see page 106). Meanwhile the public continues to demand wildlife protection. A conservation coalition is therefore suing the Canadian government for not exercising its responsibility under the *Species at Risk Act* (see page 51) to protect the caribou.[1]

LEFT: *About a third of a woodland caribou's summer diet is ground lichen and two-thirds in winter is tree lichen. It takes from 80 to 150 years for a tree to produce lichen, so the continued logging of old-growth forest is a main reason woodland caribou are in grave danger of extirpation in Alberta.*

"Robin!" A commotion 200 metres away catches my eye. "A grizzly! Charging out of the forest!"

In a flash the bulls are on their feet, ears laid back, eyes glued on the bear. Pulses racing, our hands fly to bear-spray canisters. We look desperately about for trees to climb, but see none taller than ourselves within sprinting distance.

The bear, however, has no interest in any of us. It veers off, down-meadow, bounding through willow-choked streams and sending up sheets of spray as it goes. Then it vanishes from view down the valley. Relieved, we turn back to the caribou – but they are gone.

JASPER VILLAGE DISAPPEARS IN OUR REAR-VIEW MIRROR as we head down the Icefields Parkway, one of the most scenic mountain roads in the world. The jagged peaks rekindle memories of past adventures. In summer, we've hiked alpine meadows, traversed crevasse-riddled glaciers, and climbed rocky peaks, our spirits soaring. I've skinny-dipped in ice-cold tarns, then hauled out on a rock, tingling and purified. In winter, setting out with friends in the early hours by moonlight, we've ski-toured over alpine passes and down snow slopes, finishing the day in a warm cabin or around a campfire, near treeline.

We've been overwhelmed by the beauty of the alpine: peaks brushed apricot in the glow of dawn, or red, gold, and purple in the rapture of sunset. And we've felt its wrath: snow sliding from under our skis in an avalanche; lightning crackling around us as we hurried to escape off an exposed ridge, our hair bristling and ice-axes buzzing. Such experiences have kindled in us a profound respect for Nature and our place in it.

And now something new, intimate: we're drawn to the private lives of its inhabitants, for, while harsh, the alpine is not sterile. In summer, colourful wildflowers on passes and scree slopes outsmart cold and drought by hugging the ground. Orange and yellow lichens blanket once-naked rocks and slowly dissolve them, creating soil that other plants need. The detritus

Marian takes a break on Dolomite Pass. The Dolomite Peak circuit takes you from Helen Creek to Mosquito Creek through superb mountain landscape. It's considered one of the best one-day ski tours in the Canadian Rockies.

ABOVE, TOP: *Double skulls sandwiching a bone lattice protect the brains of rutting bighorn sheep, but broken horns and cut faces are common.* BOTTOM: *Dominant rams treat others as ewes, kicking and mounting them. Success, unpunished, demonstrates dominance.*

of the plants and visiting insects and small animals add to the soil. So it goes: endless death, rebirth, and the slow evolution of a landscape.

IT'S MID-OCTOBER AND THE BIGHORN SHEEP will soon rut. Early next morning, after camping at Wilcox Creek, we hike steeply up through 400-year-old subalpine forest onto broad meadows sweeping up to Wilcox Pass. The panorama is breathtaking: Mount Athabasca, Snow Dome, Mount Kitchener, and the Athabasca Glacier. Against this superb backdrop, a band of eleven rams graze the tussock grass. We sit quietly to watch.

Bighorns are magnificent animals with large, stocky bodies and rich, grey-brown coats. Their white rumps and muzzles shine in the morning sun. The rams are calm, yet tense, for in a few weeks the rut will start. One cold November comes to mind. Four big fellas were slugging it out for dominance over a band of ewes. The largest we called Chief, as he clearly was the boss. His massive horns, tips broken, and scarred face told of numerous battles. The challengers we named Chocolate, Larry, and Dennis.

The action started mildly enough, the four standing in a huddle. Then, in slow motion, they repositioned, challengers facing Chief, who stood, muzzle held high, sizing them up. Who would be the first to take him on? None seemed anxious to try. Larry goaded Chocolate, kicking him between the forelegs, but to no avail. Chocolate then prodded Dennis, who prodded Larry.

Round and round this went until somehow Larry plucked up courage. Turning his back on Chief, he walked slowly away five or six paces, as if without a care in the world. If sheep could whistle and put front hooves in trouser pockets, Larry would have. Then, abruptly, he spun around, reared up on hind legs, tottered forward several steps, and came crashing down, hind legs flying up behind, as he butted Chief with all the force he could muster.

FACING PAGE: *Bighorns live in bands of 15 or more, centred on the ewes. Older ewes provide leadership and security to younger ewes, lambs, and immature males. For much of the year, mature rams live in bands of their own, led by the older individuals.*

ABOVE: *Rivers, agriculture, and urban areas south of Calgary depend not on glaciers but on the Rockies' snowpack, which is also shrinking.*

FACING PAGE: *The Rockies are the "water towers" of the Prairies. This sign is one of several marking the Athabasca Glacier's former extent. It helps show how much the glacier has shrunk: one third in volume and 1.5 kilometres in length over the last 150 years. The loss is irrefutable evidence of rapid climate change.*

Chief was ready for him. As Larry reared and came forward so did he, and the two massive heads collided with a crack that could be heard across the valley. With scarcely a pause, Chocolate slammed into Chief; then Dennis did the same.

Chief was unfazed. "If that's your best shot, I'm not impressed," his body language implied. Head held high, he stared unblinkingly at his challengers – who looked, well, sheepish.

The action was repeated over and over until, as the afternoon light faded, so did the challengers, who returned to grazing. And the Chief? Adrenalin pumping, he thrashed a juniper with his horns, then sauntered over to carry out a highly personal olfactory examination of a ewe.

ACROSS THE ICEFIELDS PARKWAY FROM WILCOX lies the Columbia Icefield, the largest icefield in the Rockies. Snow Dome, its summit, is the hydrographic apex of the continent. Its glaciers feed rivers flowing to the Atlantic, Pacific, and Arctic oceans, watering and nourishing the lands between. The best known of these glaciers is the Athabasca. It plunges from the icefield's northern rim, tumbles and fractures over three great rock bands, then flows down-valley to its toe. There, it feeds a tributary of the Athabasca River.

Robin and I hike the glacier's forefield – the jumbled debris dumped by its receding toe. What a shock! The glacier has retreated such a long way since first we set foot here in 1973. Around the end of the Little Ice Age in the mid-19th century, it was 7.5 kilometres long and extended clean across where the parkway is today. Since then, however, the glacier has melted faster than snow replaces it, especially in recent decades, retreating more than 1.5 kilometres and losing a third of its volume.

The Athabasca is not alone: Mike Demuth, one of Canada's leading glaciologists, says glacial cover in the North Saskatchewan River basin is the least it's been in the last 8,000 years. Matching climate-change scientists' predictions, the basin's rivers are now in mid- to long-term decline. If it is

hard to visualize global warming and its impact on the water supply the Prairie Provinces depend on, there's no better place to visit for a reality check than the Athabasca's toe.[2]

BELOW THE WORLD OF ROCK AND ICE lies the dark-green subalpine forest so characteristic of the Rockies. The seasons have turned and we're journeying through it in summer, down the parkway. Frost-free barely one month a year, it is called the snow forest because it receives more snow than any other forest in Alberta. Grassland covers its high south- and west-facing slopes. Closed forest with feathermoss underfoot covers north-facing ones. Shrubs and herbs fill avalanche paths, and mountain streams course through it all. We follow the snow forest down to the Trans-Canada Highway, then east along the Bow Valley toward Banff.

SOON CASTLE MOUNTAIN towers over us where the valley enters a montane landscape. From their eastern ranges westward, the Rockies are overwhelmingly alpine and subalpine. But it's their montane valley bottoms – some 5 percent of Banff and 7 percent of Jasper national parks – that is their life-blood. I love these places. Their lower altitude and milder climate result in an appealing patchwork of grass, wildflowers, shrubs, aspens, and Douglas-fir. Snow-eating chinook winds expose good winter grazing for elk and deer, while the varied habitat provides the shelter, birthing areas, and movement corridors critical to wildlife survival.[3]

You'd think such habitat in a national park would be safe for wildlife, but you'd be wrong. This is also where people have located towns and road and rail corridors. Road and rail kills are a serious concern. Some 205 large mammals are reported killed annually on roads in Banff, Yoho, Kootenay, and Jasper national parks combined. Add 20 percent more for unreported road kills. On average trains kill another 70 in Banff and Jasper parks (partly because grain leaked from railcars attracts hungry animals). Total: some 316 yearly.[4]

Subalpine snow forest receives more snow than any other forest in Alberta.

Jim Bertwistle of Parks Canada says trucks account for about 12 percent of vehicles on Jasper's Yellowhead Highway but almost half the roadkills. Tractor-trailers barrelling along on wet or icy mountain roads are often unable to avoid an animal that steps into the road. Indeed, the manager of a Calgary trucking company told us he advises his drivers not to swerve and risk an accident if they see an animal on the road, but to line it up with the centre of the bumper and "take it out." [5]

Parks Canada says that, in managing the Trans-Canada Highway, it must balance "three equally important goals: to improve motorist safety; reduce wildlife-traffic conflicts; and increase the efficient movement of goods and people." Accordingly, since 1980 it has been twinning and fencing the highway, and installing under- and overpasses for wildlife to cross. While acknowledging that fencing prevents wildlife from freely crossing more than 98 percent of the highway, Parks claims the policy is effective. On completed sections, traffic flow (an average of 17,000 vehicles per day) and public safety have improved and, according to ecologist Dr. Tony Clevenger, hired by Parks Canada to advise on crossing structures, roadkills are down 80 percent. [6]

Animals crossed these structures more than 84,000 times in the past 10 years, so they certainly work. But do they work well enough? Some people think it would be preferable to build long, open-span bridges or viaducts for vehicles over the major wildlife corridors, to give wildlife more crossing choices. If the experts agree that this would be a better solution, we should do it. This is a wealthy country. Habitat connectivity is important for species with small populations, and the Bow Valley is one of the most developed areas in the world where grizzlies still survive. Males must find females to mate, and females, adequate food if they are to reproduce. Most grizzlies prefer to keep well away from busy highways, so they're unlikely even to find the crossing structures. Only when more suitable habitat is taken up by other bears do some choose habitat near roads and towns – where they risk dying at the hands of humans. [7]

ABOVE, TOP: *The Steller's jay lives in the snow forests of the Rockies and is easily seen in Waterton Lakes National Park.* BOTTOM: *The white-tailed ptarmigan's plumage changes from all-white in winter, to a mottled brown in summer, to a mixture of the two in spring and fall – ideal camouflage at or above treeline.*

The larger problem for wildlife, though, isn't the effectiveness of the crossing structures, which will take time to assess, nor is it just the highway. The real issue is the cumulative effect of development and human use in these valleys. A landmark study in 1996, *Banff-Bow Valley at the Crossroads*, highlighted the ongoing struggle between the business community's desire for yet more growth and the determination of those wanting these valleys kept in a natural state.

But Parks Canada's mandate is clear. The *National Parks Act* says that the maintenance or restoration of ecological integrity "shall be the first priority of the Minister when considering all aspects of park management." Nowhere does it mention just-in-time goods delivery or ski-resort expansion, let alone make these an equal priority. If we want to maintain healthy wildlife populations, we will have to exercise restraint. We will have to stop over-promoting the mountain parks as a tourist destination and place a cap on human use. We may have to limit private vehicle access to certain places at certain times of year and move more goods by train. Studies and reports we can do. What's missing is the political courage to act decisively.

To reach Kananaskis Country, we head east from Banff along the Bow Valley to Canmore. Until 1988 a coal-mining village of 3,000, today Canmore is Canada's leading mountain outdoor recreation centre, population 14,500 and rising. But sprawling suburbs and golf courses threaten to choke off animal movement and numbers, and result in occasional cougar and bear attacks on people. In 1992, public outcry succeeded in persuading Alberta's Natural Resources Conservation Board to disallow the Three Sisters industrial tourism proposal for nearby Wind Valley, and to require corridors of natural vegetation, free of development, for wildlife movement through the Bow Valley.[8]

At the Rockies' eastern edge, we travel south on Highway 40 up the Kananaskis River valley. In 1973, we enjoyed it as wilderness. Then in 1977

ABOVE: *Banff townsite is our best-known mountain resort; but it paves over habitat and cuts off vital travel corridors for the wildlife visitors have come to see.*

FACING PAGE: *Hundreds of animals are killed, injured, or orphaned each year on Alberta's roads.*

ABOVE: *Alpine meadow below Helen Lake, Banff National Park. The meadow is home to hoary marmots, who have their burrows in nearby talus (boulder) slopes.*

FACING PAGE: *Kananaskis Country. Calgarians treasure the area for recreation; and Alberta urgently needs to manage its forests for watershed protection. Yet the government has turned over 40 percent of the Kananaskis for commercial logging.*

it was designated a provincial recreation area for strenuous physical activity from a good road, but to be relatively free of construction.

The vision didn't last. (The new moniker, "Kananaskis Country," was a clue. In British parlance, "town" and "country" alike are man-made landscapes.) K-Country today is a mishmash of provincial parks and forest lands (see page 77). It has ski hills, visitor centres, a hotel "village," two gas stations, a golf course, campgrounds, carparks, bike trails, private resorts, and an off-highway vehicle play area, and in places it bristles with city-style signage. In June 2000, under public pressure, the government rejected the huge Genesis resort proposal and created the Spray Lakes Provincial Park in its stead – for which, three cheers! But new development proposals are never far away. Under a Forest Management Agreement in 2001, the government turned over management of nearly 40 percent of K-Country to a logging company.[9]

K-Country still offers much to enjoy, though. It's a beautiful sunny day as we hike the meadow under Mt. Lorette. Here, in March 1992, Peter Sherrington made a remarkable discovery. He and fellow naturalist Des Allen were counting birds when he noticed a golden eagle. It was riding thermals above the ridge across the valley, then glided like an arrow northward. By day's end they'd seen more than 100 of the eagles – extraordinary, given that the species was thought non-migratory. Sherrington and volunteers have since counted eagles there every spring and fall. He wasn't the first to notice them, but his meticulous records have proved the existence of a major golden eagle flyway possibly unique in the world. On average, more than 3,000 are counted on their spring journey north to breed. The number exceeds 3,500 in autumn when, in early September, their fledglings appear, then the adult eagles, on the return journey to the USA and Mexico.

Not content to watch specks in the sky, Robin and I have several times hauled our camera gear up a remote mountainside, then crouched all day

in frigid October wind out of sight under the ridge top, awaiting eagles. The rewards have been unforgettable. We've been so close to many an eagle as it crested the ridge just above ground level that we have seen its surprised stare, heard the rush of wind over its wings, and distinguished the fine details of its feathers as it sailed south.

WE, TOO, HEAD SOUTH – to hike the Whaleback. Here at the foot of the Livingstone Range, from south of Chain Lakes to the Oldman River, lies the largest undisturbed expanse of montane habitat remaining in Canada. White spruce border its streams, aspens decorate river terraces, and lodgepole pine the mid-slopes. Open forests of ancient Douglas-fir clad the ridge tops, and gnarled limber pine – some over 575 years old – the rocky outcrops. Grassy southern exposures brim with wildflowers in spring. They provide snow-free winter range for mule deer and Alberta's largest elk herd, 2,000 strong. Cougar, wolverine, black and grizzly bear roam here, and 80 bird species come to nest.[10]

James Tweedie is kneading bread dough on a huge wooden table by a wood-burning stove at his ranch house. Over mugs of tea, the bearded long-time resident tells us that, while the Whaleback is, after years of lobbying, partially protected as Heritage Rangeland, the public must be constantly vigilant. In 2003, the conservation community and local ranchers fought off yet another gas-well drilling application. But the government countered by partially rolling back protection from off-highway vehicles, allowing them into the Whaleback's Bob Creek area, where none was allowed before.[11]

ABOVE: *A golden eagle flies over Kananaskis Country to its southern wintering grounds.*

FACING PAGE: *Hoary marmots are North America's largest squirrels. They live in the meadows and talus slopes of the subalpine, and survive the harsh winter season by hibernating for seven or eight months of the year. They are prey for golden eagles.*

36

FACING PAGE: *The Whaleback is the most extensive, least disturbed, and least fragmented montane landscape in Alberta. Here a delightful mix of trees and grassland spills out from the mountains over low ridges resembling the spines and ribs of whales.*

ABOVE: *Limber pine, some nearly 600 years old, are characteristic of the Whaleback.*

ABOVE: *The Castle Wilderness–Waterton area has the richest diversity of species in the province. Over half of Alberta's nearly 1,600 native vascular plants can be found in the Castle, 160 of which are provincially rare including the yellow monkeyflower.*

FACING PAGE: *After a storm at Beaver Mines Lake, South Castle.*

* Invasive plant species are a little-known but rapidly spreading threat to the integrity and value of our ecosystems. Their impact far exceeds the damage caused by wildfire, says the Alberta Invasive Plants Council. The problem is one of human activity and ignorance.

THE CASTLE WILDERNESS flanks the continental divide from Crowsnest Pass down to Waterton Lakes National Park. Once it formed part of the park, but today it is unprotected.

It is a sizzling July day as we hike the 35-kilometre round trip down the South Castle and back. We're in search of the yellow monkeyflower, which is extremely rare in Alberta. Ten hours and a sprained ankle later, we arrive back at our vehicle, satisfied. We have the beautiful flower captured on film and have seen elk, bighorn sheep, mule deer, and tracks of moose, wolf, and black bear. Cougar, grizzly bear, and wolverine, who also use the Castle, kept their presence secret. For wildlife, it seems a good place to be. But Dr. David Sheppard shakes his head. "It should be, but if animals could speak, they'd tell a different story," he reckons.

We've joined the retired professor of animal ecology over coffee at his picturesque log house fronting the mountains. His wife, Jean, stands at an easel, painting a landscape inspired by the Castle wilderness. "The Castle is special because of its high biodiversity, its rare plants and animals," he says. "From an evolutionary and biological point of view, it's a real hotspot and should be protected." But the exact opposite is happening.

"Many human activities are having a damaging effect," he points out. He cites natural gas development and the logging of what little old-growth forest remains. These industries bulldoze access roads up valleys, which increases hunting pressure, legal and illegal. Also, there's the Castle Mountain Resort.

"It threatens to block animal movement through the valleys, especially of sensitive species like grizzly bears," he says. So does widespread random camping. And summer cattle-grazing has caused timothy grass, Kentucky bluegrass, smooth brome, and weeds to replace the nutritious native grasses. Unlike the invaders,* those natives cure on the stem, hence are critical for wildlife survival in winter. "So use is piled upon use and frankly I think we are destroying the Castle."[12]

Local residents first requested legal protection for the Castle in 1968. Almost 40 years later, it has still not been granted. Many concerned groups are seeking its protection as the Andy Russell-I'tai sah kòp Wildland Provincial Park.

AS WE ENTER WATERTON LAKES NATIONAL PARK, tension slips away and peace washes over us. This is a gorgeous park and off the beaten track. When the federal government reduced its size by half in 1921, Waterton, at 525 square kilometres, became too small to encompass even one male grizzly bear's territory. Fortunately, the park is contiguous with Glacier National Park in Montana. As a result, bears, wolves, and other animals that seasonally cover great distances in search of food and mates can move safely between the two. But step outside the park and they may legally be shot by Alberta ranchers and landowners, while hunters can shoot wolves without limit.[13]

Waterton today is as delightful as ever, with splendid mountain scenery and a biological richness matching that of the Castle. This diversity results from the juncture of prairie and mountain, and from Pacific storms tracking through its valleys from British Columbia. In total, 971 vascular plant species live here, a fifth of them among Alberta's rarest and 22 found nowhere else in the province.[14]

The Pacific and central flyways overlap here, and each autumn thousands of waterfowl stop to rest before continuing south. Some 85 bird species nest in Waterton's richly varied habitats, from great blue herons to tiny calliope hummingbirds. We've seen the crested Steller's jay in the snow forest; a mountain bluebird, tree swallow, and red-shafted northern flicker squabbling over rights to a cavity nest in an aspen; pelicans performing an effortless ballet, riding thermals along the mountain front; a great horned owl patiently teaching her reluctant young to hunt prey; and a Barrow's goldeneye giving first diving lessons to hatchlings who could only bob like corks on their subalpine lake.

ABOVE: *Golden mantled ground squirrel.*

FACING PAGE: *A bull elk must constantly struggle to keep his harem together in the fall. Cows may be tempted to wander off and check out other bulls while the old man is distracted fighting off challengers or courting other cows.*

FOLLOWING PAGES: *Balsamroot blossoms are a sure sign of spring in Waterton Lakes National Park, and a tasty snack for deer.*

The light-as-a-feather scent of beargrass and the sharp, sweet taste of wild strawberries are a delight of Nature. They reawaken senses this work-a-day city dweller is apt to forget she had.

MARIAN'S DIARY, 29 JULY 2002

FACING PAGE: *Beargrass is an extraordinary waist-high lily that blooms about three years in ten. A dense cluster of small, creamy white flowers tops a stem rising from grass-like leaves. It is a favourite food of goats, bighorn sheep, deer, and elk, and in Alberta is found only in Waterton Lakes National Park.*

In wintertime, warm chinook winds bring milder temperatures and snow-free grazing for ungulates. A winter elk herd, hundreds strong, roams the low, grassy ridges and open, lakeside flats. Mule deer, white-tails, and bighorn sheep are common, attracting cougar. And Waterton is well known for bears, especially grizzlies, attracted in good berry-crop years.

"Y'ALL SEEN MO' BAY-YERS?" a now-familiar voice enquires. David Weddell from Nashville, Tennessee comes over to greet us. He is one of many who spend the time and money driving thousands of kilometres every spring and fall to see bears in action. Meanwhile, a British Elderhosteller is watching through my spotting scope as a mother black bear nurses her three cubs, then sends them up a tree for a nap. "If I'd known I'd have seen all that," he says, "I'd have paid double for my holiday!"

What is the fascination with bears? Their power? The human way they stand on two legs or nurse their young? The adrenalin rush we feel in their presence? Regardless, you need to stay alert and respectful in bear country and educate yourself about bears, for unprovoked attacks on people, while rare, do occur. They more often involve black bears, not grizzlies, and are largely due to human ignorance or carelessness. Indeed, bears mostly go out of their way to avoid humans.

We keep our distance from bears by learning their habits and using powerful spotting scopes and camera lenses from afar. Even so, we're occasionally surprised. One time, Robin was photographing a blue grouse and her brood while I scouted ahead for more picture opportunities. Rounding a bend in the trail, I came face to muzzle with a grizzly just five paces away, feeding on the far side of a saskatoon bush. For a fleeting moment our eyes met. Then, eyes cast down, I apologized softly for so rudely interrupting. The bear resumed his meal while I slowly backed down the trail and around the bend. Only then, heart thumping, did I turn and walk quickly back to Robin to share what I'd seen.

Another time, in Waterton, we were standing behind our camper watching a black bear family, upslope, eating chokecherries when a grizzly came up behind us from the valley below. Only the sound of its claws on the asphalt as it rounded our truck alerted us to its presence. We scrambled through the camper's rear door and the grizzly walked by without a second glance.

The same autumn, as we contoured a mountain slope, a grizzly emerged from some shrubs and ambled down to a pool under a small waterfall only thirty paces from us on the trail. There he sat, legs out in front, and proceeded to slosh water over his body with a massive paw. All he needed was a bar of soap to thoroughly clean up. Then he stood up, shook himself, and ambled purposefully toward us up the trail. The message was clear: "This is my home, my right of way, so move! Now!" We scrambled upslope, and he passed on his way.

The thoughtlessness of many toward bears is appalling. I recall so many hikers bear-watching along a stretch of trail that they effectively prevented a grizzly from crossing it and reaching the river, where he obviously wanted to go. When I called out, asking people to give him space, some did, others scowled at me, and one shouted: "Not 'til I've got my picture of it!"

ON THE DRIVE HOME, Robin and I take stock. We ponder our encounters with Dave Weddell, the Elderhosteller, and the Tonquin horse party, and how Kurt had called the living landscape of the Canadian Rockies a paradise.

Our own self-centred perception of the Rockies as a place merely to play and renew ourselves on weekends changed drastically long ago. Sure, people need exercise, recreation, and spiritual renewal. But Robin and I also now understand that, for so many other species, the Rockies are the only home they have left. We humans have taken almost all the rest.

Since the grizzly needs so much room to roam, the health of the grizzly population is a measure of the health of these wildlands. So back home we call Dr. Tracey Henderson, chair of the Grizzly Bear Alliance, and ask how grizzlies are faring in Alberta. Most data on grizzly populations have now

ABOVE: *Grizzly bears use or cross footpaths on their daily rounds. Caution and respect ensure safety for all and memorable views of these magnificent animals.*

FACING PAGE: *Bow Valley grizzlies reproduce less often than any in North America: the sows don't breed until age six and have cubs on average once in four years. The likely cause is too much construction and human use in habitat that is marginal compared to the bears' historic prairie range.*

been collected, she says, and we now have strong DNA evidence that there are fewer than 500 grizzlies all told in Alberta – likely under 320 within provincial jurisdiction plus 160 to 180 in Alberta's mountain national parks. Only about half are mature breeding bears. That is very few.

Alberta scientists use the standards of the World Conservation Union (IUCN) to assess the conservation status of this province's wildlife populations. Put simply, if the estimated number of mature breeding individuals in a population of large mammals falls below 1,000, the animal should be legally designated as threatened, and below 250, as endangered. Accordingly in Alberta, Henderson says, "The science is clear: the grizzly should be listed as endangered.[15]

"Yet the Alberta government refuses to accept the 2002 recommendation of its own Endangered Species Conservation Committee to list the grizzly." Why? Because once they admit there's a problem, they will come under public pressure to fix it. So, she says, "the government will likely continue to stall on that decision for years to come. The only good news is that they have finally bowed to public pressure and placed a three-year moratorium on grizzly hunting."

But hunting is not the biggest problem for grizzlies, only the easiest to deal with. Landscape ecologist Dr. J. Brad Stelfox and others point to the huge growth in human disturbance within and flanking the central Rockies as the big issue – notably resource extraction, livestock grazing on public land, recreational use, acreages, and road density and use. Little secure habitat remains where a grizzly can raise her family without encountering people or risking human-caused death. Stelfox predicts that business-as-usual could see grizzlies vanish from the Whaleback area within 50 years.[16]

Frankly, says Henderson, "wildlife would be a lot better off in Alberta, indeed across Canada, if important conservation decisions like this were made by scientists and not by politicians."

LEFT: *Mountain lady's slipper.*

Poorly is the only honest answer. In effect, the *Canadian Constitution* divides responsibility for protecting wildlife between the federal government and the provinces and territories. Under the *Accord for the Protection of Species at Risk 1996,* all these governments agreed to enact laws that, among other things: identify endangered and threatened species, afford them immediate legal protection, protect their habitat, implement recovery plans in a timely fashion, and provide effective enforcement.[17]

Canada: The *Species at Risk Act (SARA,* 2002) is the key federal law supposedly protecting endangered species. *SARA* designates species in top-down degree of risk as extinct, extirpated (meaning locally extinct), endangered, threatened, of special concern, not at risk, or requiring further study. Under *SARA,* the Committee on the Status of Endangered Wildlife in Canada (COSEWIC) - an independent scientific body - recommends to the federal government what plants and animals are at risk across Canada as a whole and their status. But it is the federal Cabinet, not COSEWIC scientists, that decides if a species will in fact be listed, and its designation.[18]

Worse, while *SARA* provides strong protection to a listed species and to its "residence" (nest or den), it doesn't protect its habitat, and it applies only to federal lands (national parks, military bases, Indian reserves, airports, and penitentiaries) - a mere 5 percent of Canada.

SARA doesn't automatically protect species at risk on private or provincial public land; it leaves that to the provinces. If, however, a province fails to protect a species listed by *SARA,* a safety-net provision gives the federal environment minister the authority to issue an emergency order to protect that species and its habitat. This may sound reassuring, but in practice the minister has refused to exercise this authority in the case of Alberta's woodland caribou and British Columbia's spotted owl, both of which face extirpation. So of what use is it?

Alberta: More than a decade after signing the accord, Alberta still has no stand-alone endangered species law. Instead, it has amended its *Wildlife Act,* really a hunting-control act, to prohibit the killing or capturing of species listed as endangered or threatened, and to prohibit disturbance to their nests or dens. But it doesn't protect their critical habitat, and the process for listing species is flawed. A scientific subcommittee makes recommendations to the Endangered Species Conservation Committee - a multi-stakeholder (predominantly industry) group - which then makes recommendations to the minister.[19]

Northern leopard frog.

Action on those recommendations, however, is left to ministerial discretion, and so far, the minister has not followed the committee's recommendation to list the grizzly bear as threatened. And even were he to do so, he is not legally required to ensure that the resulting recovery plan is acted on. So, our government's "commitment" under the accord is meaningless. The Alberta government provides little or no effective protection for endangered and threatened species, because that requires protecting their habitat.[20]

> *"We stand guard over works of art,*
> *but species representing the work of eons*
> *are stolen from under our noses."*
>
> ALDO LEOPOLD (1887-1948), ECOLOGIST,
> FORESTER, ENVIRONMENTALIST

THE GRASSLANDS

Honed by the Wind

Marian White

"COME ON! WHAT'S KEEPING YOU?" Robin's voice reaches me from the front door. I can hear *Song Dog*'s diesel engine throbbing on the driveway.

"COM-ing! Just tidying up." I finish in the kitchen, grab my car keys off the white-tail antler in the hall, lock the front door, and jump into the truck. Ready!

It's a new season and we're off down the road, to explore the grasslands of ...

"Stop!"

"What now?"

"I've forgotten my sunglasses." Robin rolls his eyes skywards. We return and I retrieve the glasses.

"OK, you're done?"

"OK."

"OK." We're off again.

Minutes later we're back. Rob has forgotten his driver's licence.

FACING PAGE: *A rainbow plunges over the breaks along the northern rim of the Milk River Canyon, in Alberta's southernmost grasslands.*

53

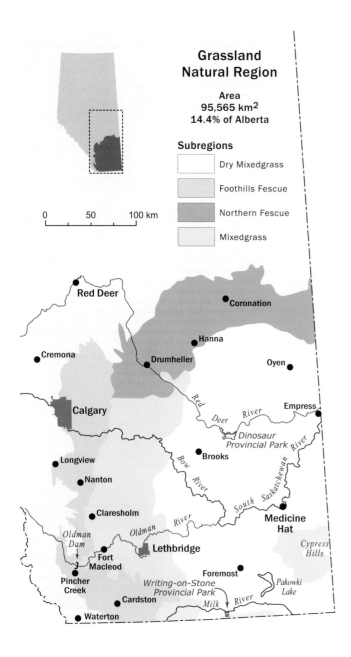

Grassland
Natural Region

Area
95,565 km²
14.4% of Alberta

Subregions

    Dry Mixedgrass

    Foothills Fescue

    Northern Fescue

    Mixedgrass

0   50   100 km

Red Deer

Coronation

Cremona

Hanna

Drumheller

Oyen

Calgary

Red Deer River

Empress

Dinosaur Provincial Park

Longview

Brooks

Nanton

Bow River

South Saskatchewan River

Claresholm

River

Oldman Dam

Oldman

Medicine Hat

Cypress Hills

Fort Macleod

Lethbridge

Foremost

Pincher Creek

Writing-on-Stone Provincial Park

Pakowki Lake

Cardston

Milk River

Waterton

This time, we tick everything off on a checklist. Finally we're away, heading east across Calgary, then rolling through farmland under an open sky. The tension subsides – it's spring and good to get away! I give Robin's thigh a squeeze. He's my pal.

PLANS FOR OUR GRASSLAND EXPLORATIONS had germinated one winter, around the fire. Stick a compass-point into Alberta's southeastern corner and inscribe an arc clockwise from the U.S. border near Cardston, up through the middle of Calgary, and around the Neutral Hills to the Saskatchewan border and there you have it, more or less: the Grassland Natural Region.

This droughty expanse of land in the rain shadow of the Rockies was, until European settlement, an ocean of grass. Its four subregions reflect subtle variations in moisture and temperature – warm and dry south and east; relatively cooler and moister north and west, with chinook winds making the western winters less chill. Short and medium-height grasses have responded to those growing conditions by evolving into distinct communities.

The region evolved in concert with more than climate alone, however. Unlike trees and most other plants, which grow from their tips, grass grows from its base at or just below ground. Out on the plains, under pressure from fire and grazing by bison (only approximated by cattle today), grasses rule supreme. Without those pressures, woody shrubs such as sagebrush encroach.[1]

Historically, the region is the western part of the triangle Captain John Palliser described around 1860 as desert-like and "unsuited for civilization."

FACING PAGE: *Silver sagebrush in Dinosaur Provincial Park. This drought-resistant woody shrub affords nutritious winter food, shelter from hot summers and bitter winters, and nesting sites. Hence, it is vital for pronghorns and many birds, including long-billed curlews, sage sparrows, and the endangered sage-grouse and sage thrasher. Park aside, this habitat is dwindling and needs protection.*[2]

54

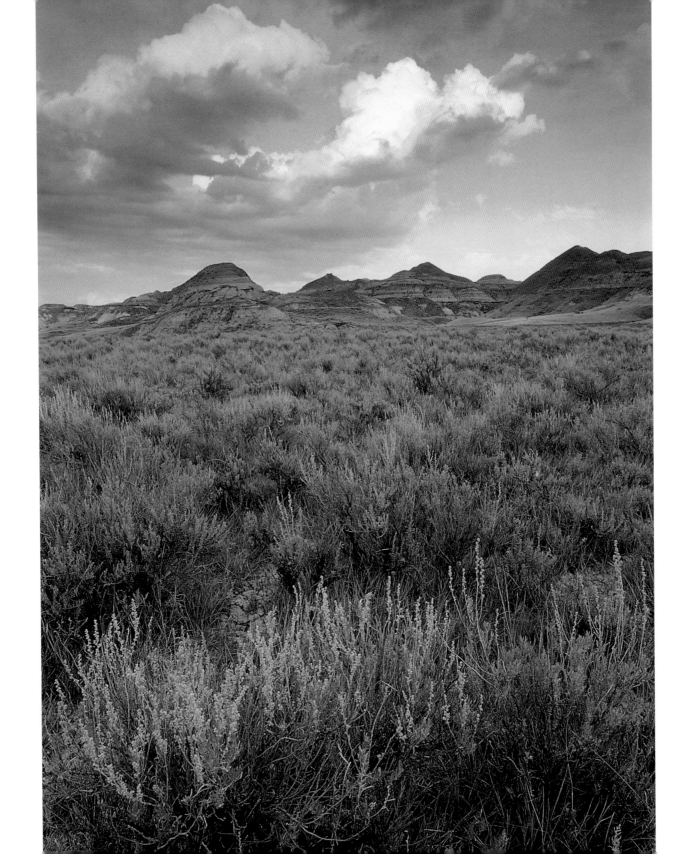

Yet by 1920 a single generation of homesteading immigrants had ploughed up 80 percent of that native grassland. [3]

This Robin and I knew. But to sketch out our plan, we had to learn how much native grassland remains and where to find it. If anyone knew, it would be Cliff Wallis, a highly respected grassland biologist and international consultant. The soft-spoken Calgarian is a champion of Alberta's wildlife and wildlands.

So, as winter waned, we had visited Wallis and sat at the boardroom table in his basement, surrounded by filing cabinets stuffed to overflowing. Wallis had fished out a map showing the remaining contiguous expanses of native grassland. What a shock! The region's central and western areas were almost blank. Our best bet, he said, would be the 5,000-square-kilometre Milk River/Sage Creek borderlands – largely federal and provincial grazing reserves. Most of Alberta's rare and endangered grassland species survive there. Wallis also suggested other places and species to see, and soon a plan emerged.

Now, IT'S SPRING and we're on the road. First on our itinerary will be the Foothills Fescue Subregion. Here we'll birdwatch lakes and sloughs east of Calgary, then head to Foremost, our Dry Mixedgrass base camp. From there, we'll explore Pakowki Lake for its sand dunes and rare plants, the grass communities of the borderlands, and Writing-On-Stone Provincial Park for wildlife among the hoodoos. Next, to Milk River Ridge and the Cardston area, back in the Foothills Fescue. By that time it will be high summer and we'll take a break in the mountains.

September will find us sampling the Northern Fescue near Coronation. Then southeast to Empress near the Saskatchewan border, followed by

LEFT: *The American avocet, shown here, once bred as far north as the Northwest Territories but now only to the boreal forest's southern edge. Its bill is ideal for skimming food from shallow water or muddy shores.* [4]

a southern loop through the desertlike Middle Sandhills – home to that prairie icon, the pronghorn, and to endangered mammals and lizards. From there we'll head west to cottonwood forest at Dinosaur Provincial Park. Finally, we'll wind our way through Lethbridge to Waterton, where our grassland journey will end. It's a rather circuitous route but will allow us to see plants and animals at their seasonal best or when most easily viewed.

MCELROY SLOUGH is one of many wetlands from Calgary to Brooks. Thousands of birds use these marshes and local lakes and reservoirs as stopover places on migration or for nesting and raising young. We pull off the road at McElroy, just north of Chestermere, and dig out our binoculars.

Watching waterfowl is like watching a soap opera: the characters, the drama, the amorous goings on! Even non-amorous behaviour can be mind-boggling. I write in my field notebook:

> *Coot are constructing ramps to their nests, which rise*
> *and fall with changing water levels. And Wilson's phalaropes*
> *are spinning in the shallows like whirligigs, up to 60 revolutions*
> *a minute. Are they crazy?*
>
> *Nope. Each bird is creating a vortex that brings to the*
> *surface small invertebrate food items, which it seizes with*
> *a needle-like beak.*

We stroll around the slough, observing diving ducks and shorebirds, meadowlarks and northern harriers living their lives in what has been called the best surviving patch of native prairie near Calgary – defined by that precious bunchgrass, rough fescue (see page 61).

RIGHT: *The male marsh wren sings and builds nests all summer long and destroys the nests of rival males.*

WONDERFUL WETLANDS

Marshes are wetlands that are part-time under water and part-time dry – sloughs, as they are called in Alberta, and the borders of cattails and sedge surrounding ponds and the shallow bays of lakes. As part of Alberta's natural capital, they provide important ecological services free of charge: they create wildlife habitat, purify and store water, control flooding, recharge groundwater, offer

us recreational and educational experiences, and create beauty in our lives.

Yet about half of Alberta's wetlands had disappeared by 1960 and 60 percent by 1999, mostly drained for agricultural and other industrial development. The margins of about 93 percent of those that remain have been degraded by agricultural practices. About 90 percent of the wetlands engulfed by Calgary have been destroyed. In 2004, to its credit, Calgary became the first North American city with a wetland protection plan.

According to Pembina Institute studies, the cumulative loss of wetland services represents economic benefits lost to Albertans worth at least $7.7 billion per year.[5]

The endangered greater sage-grouse has declined continent-wide. But declines of up to 92 percent in its Alberta population are the worst, with eight leks (courting grounds) destroyed since 1968. The largest recent habitat change is due to oil and gas development: firms have disturbed at least six leks, four of which grouse have abandoned. The associated roads and fences bring disturbance by people, including birdwatchers and photographers; fatal collisions with vehicles; and predation by perching raptors. Today, grouse use only 9 of 33 remaining Alberta leks; breeding is often interrupted, and grouse numbers are falling.[7]

THE CLEAN, SHARP SCENT OF SAGE AFTER RAIN is one of the joys of the prairie. I pinch a leaf between finger and thumb and breathe in. Its astringency clears and invigorates the mind. I'm not alone in my passion for sage: grouse, pronghorn, and other species depend on it for survival.

After several days birding sloughs and camping along the way, we leave the Trans-Canada Highway at Brooks, cut south to Highway 61, and camp at Foremost. The village is our favourite springboard for prairie exploration: local people are friendly and the place uncrowded. Today, after a bowl of Robin's delicious homemade granola, we made a dawn start and are now overlooking sagebrush and rangeland near Pakowki Lake. I recall the first time we saw sage-grouse lekking here:

23 April – The din at 4:40 a.m. woke us instantly. Quietly, Robin slid his long lens through a flap in the tent wall and I readied the tape-recorder. Outside in a classic spring ritual, cocks strutted on their lek, an open site among the brush inherited for courting.

The cocks have attitude! A handsome fellow raised his spiked fan of a tail. Then "swish" went his wings! "Pop, pop!" Air from inflated chest-sacs exploded from his beak as he strutted his stuff. I counted 34 cocks and 2 hens, the last to be fertilized.

But my memories are bittersweet, for the lek is still there but the grouse are gone. Because the species is now endangered in Alberta, the Grasslands Naturalists of Medicine Hat no longer visit the leks in season, nor tell anyone their locations.[6]

At noon, we head for the hamlet of Manyberries. There, a group of grouse researchers in a yard off the dusty street are talking shop over coffee and sandwiches. Cameron Aldridge sits among them, his navy coveralls sun-bleached from long hours working in this semi-desert. We chat about the bird. Then, pushing his sunglasses up over the peak of his baseball cap, he fixes us with dark-brown eyes.

"The greater sage-grouse," he says, "[is] becoming so weakened, it could be taken out by West Nile virus." His message? In the end, he says, it will survive only if the public decide sage-grouse are worth saving and speak out loud enough to convince our politicians to properly protect its habitat. If this fails, Alberta's sage-grouse will likely be gone by 2020.[8]

AT PAKOWKI LAKE, the southeast's largest water body, we spend days walking the dunes and watching wildlife feed their young: skunk, mule deer, Swainson's hawk, and the white-faced ibis – a bird rare in Alberta. A long-billed curlew stalks grasshoppers on a hillside.

Next day it's time to penetrate deeper into the Dry Mixedgrass. Trundling out of Foremost, we head for the Lost River/Sage Creek country in the southeast corner of the province. I'm apprehensive about this: will I see grass as just grass, the place boring, minimalist?

Nature does not disappoint. While the Rockies are in-your-face exciting, the dry-grass plains are subtle as vintage wine. This is ranching country, too dry for agriculture. The Dry Mixedgrass supports the richest diversity of wildlife in the Grassland Region, but you have to stop, walk out into it, wait and watch to experience it.

A rancher kindly lets us camp in his yard, then whets our appetite with news: mountain plovers have returned, garter snakes are about, and the first yucca is blooming. At 9 p.m., coyotes sing their intention to go a-hunting and we turn in early for the night.[9]

Up at daybreak, we head out across the huge ranch to explore. Meadowlarks flute liquid melodies from fenceposts, and McCown's longspurs engage in aerial combat. Horned larks sing way up in the sky, and flocks of them on the track scatter only milliseconds ahead of our vehicle. I'm hooked.

VROOM! AT DUSK ONE EVENING, I'm sitting on crunchy native pasture, tape-recording nighthawks. Vroom! A male hurtles down toward me, the

Newborn mule-deer fawns are relatively helpless and rely on their mottled coat, lack of scent, and keeping still to conceal them from predators. Only after about three weeks do they start travelling about with their mother.

ABOVE AND RIGHT: *The soapweed yucca ranges from Texas just into Alberta. It co-evolved in a symbiotic relationship with the yucca moth: the yucca depends solely on the moth for pollination, while the moth depends solely on the yucca flowers as a nursery and food source for its young. The grubs eventually descend on silken threads to the ground and overwinter in the soil. There they may stay for several years, awaiting a good flowering year to emerge as adult moths.*

air rushing through his primary wing feathers creating that "sonic boom." He rounds out of the dive at the last minute and heads back up, just a few feet away. I'm thrilled! This is territorial behaviour: the nighthawks' "nest" sites, mere patches of ground, must be nearby.

There's a paucity of trees for nesting in, out here on the plains. Another bird's solution is to nest underground in ground squirrel holes. It's the endangered burrowing owl. We watch a mother owl standing at her burrow entrance, with nine owlets lined up, facing her. She stretches a wing and leg. A fluffball copies her. Her mate brings her a grasshopper and she doles it out to their young. Burrowing owls are great consumers of grasshoppers, which can provide some 90 percent of their daily food items – around 14 per owl per day. One day, her mate demonstrates flying technique to the young. Two weeks later at twilight, the parents fly off and perch on adjacent fence posts. One by one, each youngster copies the flight and lands on a post. Our last sight of them as we head for camp is a row of owls along the fenceline getting ready for nocturnal mouse-hunting lessons.[10]

A colonial nester once common in the western provinces, this owl has been almost extirpated here, and surviving pairs nest alone. Many landowners care: over 700 Canadians – 200 in Alberta – are now burrowing owl habitat stewards, and owl numbers have risen a little to about 107 pairs, due to this program and owl reintroductions. But much of their remaining habitat now lies unoccupied. Why? The reasons are complex and not fully understood. They likely include disturbance, drought, and the war on ground squirrels, whose abandoned burrows they require. Unless things change, this delightful owl will vanish from Canada within 20 years.[11]

FOLLOWING PAGES: *Evolving on the treeless plains, the endangered burrowing owl uses abandoned burrows, mostly of ground squirrels, for nesting and hiding from predators. The owl is in serious decline, likely due to a complex mix of reasons.*

61

GRASSLAND COMMUNITIES

Alberta has 149 native grasses. They form diverse local mixes, some species flourishing one year, others another, depending on grazing pressure and weather. Unlike non-native species such as crested wheatgrass, timothy, or smooth brome, the natives provide ecological stability and, since they cure on the stem, nourishing winter food for wildlife and cattle.[12]

The dainty blue grama and scratchy needle-grasses dominate Dry Mixedgrass areas, while wheatgrasses replace blue grama in Mixedgrass areas. Rough fescue tussocks dominate the Northern Fescue but in the Foothills Fescue, it co-dominates with Idaho fescue and oat grasses.

In 2003, rough fescue became Alberta's official grass. There's more here than anywhere else at all, but it's under intense pressure, dwindling, and can't be restored. So it's our duty as Albertans to ensure its survival for generations to come.

ABOVE: *Severe summer storms on the prairies can bring life-giving rain, destructive tornadoes, or nothing but wind and an empty promise.*

FACING PAGE: *Writing-on-Stone Provincial Park harbours amazing aboriginal rock art and is rich in grassland plant and animal species, from rattlesnakes and turkey vultures to giant wild rye and the fragrant eveningstar, whose flowers open only at dusk.*

A VIOLENT ELECTRIC STORM BREAKS AROUND US. After many days at ranches and the Milk River canyon area, we had returned to Foremost to rest and restock. Now we're off again, seemingly the only vehicle on the road. I cling to the steering wheel, thrilled and terrified as the gale hits broadside, rain lashes down, roadside ditches overflow, thunder crashes, and the world turns pitch black. Not until crackling fork lightning strafes the sky and sheet lightning briefly lights up everything can I see the way ahead. We arrive exhausted at a campsite, eat a quick chowder, and retire to our sleeping bags, awestruck at the colossal spectacle of prairie weather.

Witnessing such raw violence connects us to the truth: that natural forces can be overwhelming. The experience leaves me feeling humble and deeply respectful of Nature.

WRITING-ON-STONE PROVINCIAL PARK is an excellent example of a Dry Mixedgrass community, and Albertans would be right to expect it to be protected. But in the mid-1990s the government began privatizing management of our park campgrounds. And at Writing-on-Stone much of the precious riverine bird habitat, where the campground is situated, was destroyed to make way for more campsites for added profit. The government has since taken back control – but the habitat has yet to be restored. Campground aside, though, the park remains one of my favourites.[13]

It is early morning and I'm sitting on a rock among the hoodoos, witnessing an extraordinary thing. Four brown-headed cowbirds have just flown in from nearby grassland and are engaging in a ritual square dance on a tall, flat-topped pillar. Each in turn spreads its wings, bows, and displays to the others. Next, two display to each other, then jump up and down, beak to beak. Finally, the four take turns displaying to all once more; then they fly back to the grassland to feed. I'm overawed at this rare insight into their world.

The yellow-flowered prickly pear cactus likes dry clay soil or eroded areas, while the pink-flowered pincushion cactus (not shown) prefers stony ground.

Time to leave. I hunt down Robin and find him sprawled on a grassy slope, photographing a cottontail who's gotten so used to him it might as well have been on a posing stand.

"'Bye, bunny." We're off, out of the Dry Mixedgrass and west to Milk River Ridge in the Foothills Fescue. We eat supper by the reservoir – a campground inhabited by so many voluble robins and kingbirds that we hardly notice the people. Eventually the wind in the trees sighs us all to sleep.

MILK RIVER RIDGE SURPRISES ME. This divide between the Saskatchewan and Missouri drainages is higher than I had imagined. We explore on foot. It's beautiful. On the hilltops and slopes, a profusion of colourful wildflowers is blooming among tussocky rough fescue. We meet Roger Thompson of the local grazing association out riding the range.

"This is a very special place, you know – a refugium. It didn't get glaciated, so rare plants have survived here." As Thompson tells us about the ridge with pride, a rancher stops by in a pickup.

"The government manages this Natural Area very well," he says, referring to the strict regimen imposed upon those permitted to graze this public land. "Contrast that with the ranchers. These last four drought years, they've overgrazed their own land."

Ranchers are interested in plants but sometimes ambivalent toward wild animals. Having wildlife around is part of the ranching experience they enjoy so much. But some draw a line at grizzly bears.

"They come right out here from the mountains," the man says, "and I don't like 'em. My policy with them is the three S's: shoot, shovel, and shut up."

Not amused, we head back to *Song Dog* and drive through the Foothills Fescue to a campground in Cardston, where we spend the night.

AS A CHILD IN ENGLAND, I never knew where irises came from – or other garden flowers, for that matter. Oh, yes, I helped Mum plant bulbs, but no one ever told me of the cultivars' origins in the wild. For me, wildflowers grew in the woods and garden bulbs came from the garden centre. Now here am I, decades later, down in the moist Foothills Fescue, kneeling in a rancher's meadow by some wild irises – the western blue flag.

Its flowers are smaller than I expected. Ah, but of course they are because, among other things, horticulturists selectively breed cultivars to produce bigger blooms. So we urban folk see Nature through a distorted lens.

The irises look vulnerable in the lush grass, and so they are. These wildflower meadows are breathtakingly beautiful – to my city mind, heaven on earth. Yet when we knock on his door to say thanks to the rancher, he smiles wryly and recalls years of drought.

"I call this country 'Next Year Land'," he says.

"Then how is it your meadows are so healthy, so brimming with wildflowers?"

"Well you see, for 20 years I've had the cattle graze the blue flag pastures only winter and fall." That way, his cattle are well fed but don't overgraze the site; they eat enough competing grass but not the iris; and they fertilize the superb diversity Nature offers. Both cattle and iris flourish. It's called reciprocity. It has to do with love and respect for the land.

All I can say is, hats off to those ranchers who care deeply enough that, despite government foot-dragging, they preserve the nation's wild heritage on their land. Society needs to publicly honour such good stewards. And Robin and I like to reward good stewards by buying local, organically grown meat and vegetables. Such action puts money directly into the hands of local farmers and supports the local economy.

Shaking hands, we bid the rancher farewell. It's time for an August break in the mountains, before part two of our grassland journey.

"WE NEVER SAW MUCH WILDLIFE when we were kids," says dark-haired, 40-something Dylan Biggs. It's September and we're back on the Great

The beautiful, slender iris called the blue flag survives at a few sites in Alberta, mostly close to the United States border, in swampy wetland of the Grassland's Foothills Fescue Subregion. Neither this nor any other plant species has been protected under Alberta law .

PLANTS LIVE DANGEROUSLY IN ALBERTA!

In Canada the blue flag, a wild iris, occurs only in southernmost Alberta, at the northern edge of its range. By 1998, more than half the handful of reported sites had been destroyed or altered. So in 2001, the iris was approved for listing as threatened under the provincial *Wildlife Act*.[16]

Problem! The blue flag never actually made it to that legal list. So far, the government has developed regulations (tools needed to carry out an Act) only for the conservation of animals, not plants. Development of plant regulations did begin but they are still in limbo.

Recent surveys have found a total of 18 blue flag sites, all but two on private land. Officials and most landowners are collaborating to protect them. Alberta likes to think itself a leader, but in lacking legal protection for plants, it lags behind the federal government. And lacking a compensation program for landowners who protect "at risk" species and vital habitat, it lags way behind the U.K. and U.S.[17]

Plains. Biggs is showing us around the family's award-winning, organic TK Ranch near Coronation, in the cooler Northern Fescue Subregion at the apex of Palliser's Triangle.

The flood of settlers in the early 20th century overpopulated the prairie way beyond carrying capacity, Biggs explains. Alberta's driest areas (most of the grassland north of Brooks and east of Drumheller) were home to only 75 people in 1901, rocketing to nearly 30,000 by 1932. Meanwhile, drought and mismanagement saw half the topsoil blow away and the Depression hit. Municipalities collapsed and most settlers fled. Only about 5,300 remain today. "Those who hung on survived the 1940s and '50s by hunting for subsistence," he says. So the wildlife was all shot out.[14]

"But today few hunt. So wildlife has come back. We're seeing lots of eagles, foxes, mule deer, white-tails, thirteen-lined ground squirrels, snowy owls, pronghorns...."[15]

The demanding land this man has loved so much is virgin prairie, "saved from the plough by all the rocks," he says. He coaxes a living from it, raising pure pasture-fed, unadulterated livestock for the rapidly growing health-food market. And he encourages, and markets for, like-minded ranchers. We buy his meat every week because it's food we know we can trust.

But drought has taken its toll on Biggs and the fescue. Now, he manages his herd to graze each area just once each year to give the land, and himself, a rest. He and his family will survive, for he has other strings to his bow. And he cares about the land and treats it with respect.

BUOYED BY GOOD FEELINGS, Robin and I continue our journey, via Oyen to the Red Deer River at Empress, near the Saskatchewan border. Here, Wallis had said, we'd find some of the best riverine landscape in the grasslands. He's right. Cottonwood forest flanks the meanders. A great blue heron is still-fishing in the shallows and four mule deer leave the cottonwoods and wade across the river to browse. A porcupine waddles down the bank and drinks at the water's edge.

A side trip down Highway 41 to Sandy Point winds through the stark Middle Sandhills landscape to the South Saskatchewan River. It's hot and dry and I feel like Crocodile Dundee in an outback oasis, camping here. The autumn colours of the sparse cottonwood stands are spectacular. Migrating warblers flit through the riverside shrubs. And rattlesnakes are around, says the campground hostess – lots of them!

Driving west now, on Highway 555, we scout for pronghorn along the edge of the sandhills. But they are elusive and can travel super-fast – nearly 100 kilometres an hour, tops. And travel they do – sometimes over 400 kilometres to escape cruel winters or March storms that can kill up to half their fawns. Increasing gas-well and other disturbance in southern Alberta, and growing scarcity of water that supports their forage, mean protection of vital corridors linking suitable summer and winter range is urgently needed.

After a few fleeting sightings, our route winds down from the high plains through badlands to a broad river terrace. This is Dinosaur Provincial Park, but we're seeking wildlife, not fossils.

A footpath leads us across sagebrush flats to cottonwood forest bordering the Red Deer River. I recall one June there: female cottonwoods shedding their seeds, creating great "snowdrifts," and a sparrow landing and vanishing in the fluff; splendid carpets of golden bean; and a mallard tending her nest under a rosebush. Paradise. Or is it?

No young cottonwoods are replacing old here (or along the Bow River). A government sign alludes to the cause of the problem as "water development projects upstream," meaning the Dickson Dam. "This habitat needs your help," pleads the beleaguered signwriter.

Help? After a few days enjoying Dinosaur, we drive south to learn more from leading cottonwood scientist Stewart Rood, at the University of Lethbridge. Today, he tells us, 89 dams and weirs block southern Alberta's rivers – mainly in the Oldman and Bow drainages, overwhelmingly to irrigate farmland – so cottonwoods were in deep trouble. "Ninety percent below the

The pronghorn is a living grassland icon. When Europeans destroyed the bison, desperate natives switched to hunting pronghorn, almost to extirpation. Two temporary Alberta national parks aided pronghorn recovery, and today a million pronghorn roam the plains, some 17,000 in Alberta alone.[18]

ABOVE: *Mature cottonwood trees and golden bean border the Red Deer River.*

FACING PAGE: *The badlands of Dinosaur Provincial Park, a World Heritage Site, are one of the world's two most important sources of dinosaur fossils. Golden eagles, swallows, rock wrens, and mountain bluebirds nest here.*

St. Mary [an Oldman tributary] Dam have died because mature trees need decent summer flows to survive." [19]

When the Alberta government began building the Three Rivers (now called the Oldman) Dam illegally (1986-1991), the matter went to court. This didn't stop the dam, but the adverse public reaction did lead to the government's funding Rood's cottonwood research. His discovery? Dam operators must let flow rates decline gradually after a flood, because groundwater level falls at the same rate as the river level. For cottonwood seedlings to get established, it is critical that the groundwater not recede faster than the seedlings' roots can grow to tap into it. [20]

So the government began operating some dams accordingly and in 1995 Nature helped with a flood of a size seen only once in over 100 years. "This resulted in countless seedlings getting established on the St. Mary," says Rood, "and billions along the Oldman and South Saskatchewan." Also, the effect of the Dickson Dam on the Red Deer River's cottonwoods is under study. Clearly, it pays for the public to keep up the pressure to protect our environment. [21]

BUT WE MUST ACT FAST, for a rapidly growing water crisis looms. Eighty percent of us live in Alberta's semi-arid southern half and we are multiplying fast. Yet unlike Australians or Israelis we squander water.

Furthermore, "the [most urgent threat to] our water supply is climate warming," says freshwater expert Dr. David Schindler. Most of Alberta is one to four degrees warmer than 50 years ago, he notes, and evaporation increases with temperature, further intensifying drought So it's no surprise, he says, that with climate warming, drought, water withdrawals, dams – which increase evaporation, and more people and livestock, "we've seen a decline in every river in Alberta." The summer flow of the Oldman declined 57 percent and the South Saskatchewan 84 percent from 1912 to 2003. [22]

For years the government has allocated users more water from our southern rivers than they often contain in summer. So, many already suffer

shortages and Calgary likely will within a decade. Also nearly half Canada's worst water quality examples are in southern Alberta. If not enough water is left for the rivers themselves and we remove Nature's filters – wetland depressions and riverside greenery – the rivers can't cope with the pollution we pour into them. Aquifers and wells are put at risk. People sicken. Fish die. And dams prevent the threatened bull trout (our official provincial fish) and other fish from reaching their former spawning grounds upstream.

In 2003, our government appeared to see the light when it created the *Water for Life* strategy, full of good ideas. Then a provincial water council and watershed public advisory councils for the South Saskatchewan, Bow, and Oldman basins were set up. Further public pressure led in August 2006 to a moratorium on issuance of new water licences for those basins.

But it's too early to celebrate. Authorities still promote more diversions and water consuming industries such as intensive livestock operations and the recently approved billion-dollar super-mall and racetrack at Balzac in the Bow basin. What's wrong is a lack of strategic planning for Alberta's increasingly stretched water resources. And water, formerly a right, is now a commodity for sale to the highest bidder.

"It is time," Schindler says, "for Albertans to address the question of how much industry and human population we want." [23]

Leaving Lethbridge, we head south to the Cardston campground once more. After supper eaten in frustrated silence, we plan tomorrow's trip and retire for the night in the fine old cottonwood stand.

If you stand quietly on a rainy day in spring at the edge of a pond or dugout in Alberta's prairie or parkland, you may be lucky enough to see a tiger salamander (above).

Spring is when the adults leave their dryland burrows nearby to breed in the shallow water. But this neotenic individual never left the pond. It reached adult size and sexual maturity while retaining its larval form – note those large, external gills!

FACING PAGE: *Ancient cottonwoods line a swale (former river channel) in Dinosaur Provincial Park by the Red Deer River. Some 95 percent of southern Alberta's formerly abundant cottonwood groves were destroyed by pioneers. Today, cottonwood forest is the most threatened type of forest in North America.*

Half of Dinosaur's more than 160 bird species depend on the cottonwoods. Cottonwoods feed and shelter wildlife, "including a zillion insects whose larvae inhabit the river and become food for fish and birds," says Lorne Fitch of Alberta's Cows and Fish Program.[24]

A HERD OF 17 SHAGGY BEASTS wanders slowly, cropping the grass. These are not cattle but plains bison. The dominant bull's massive square head, black woolly crown, and long, spade-like black beard remind me of carvings of Sumerian warriors. Two younger bulls roll on their backs with abandon, legs in the air, enjoying sandbaths in scoops the herd has made on a sunny hillside. Several youngsters frolic with the sheer joy of being alive.

Bison evolved hand in glove with grass and ground squirrels. But Robin and I aren't watching a wild herd roaming a vast native prairie. This is a remnant confined to a compound we're driving through this morning, at Waterton Lakes National Park. The bison's plight results from a horror story of human greed, politics, and violence, culminating around 1889 in the extinction of free-roaming herds in the wild. Parks Canada in Alberta championed bison preservation in 1907 by giving survivors a home. Today, their rare, purebred descendants live on in Elk Island National Park, east of Edmonton – and some offspring of those, in Waterton. But most herds you see today are commercial beefalo: bison crossed at least twice with cattle to render this dangerous animal manageable. Even most conservation herds are thus contaminated.[25]

Lately, Nature Conservancy Canada and others are envisioning an intact prairie ecosystem evolving anew, with bison once again freely roaming the plains. In December 2003, they began reintroducing purebred descendants of the refugees in Elk Island to Old Man on His Back, a protected native grassland in southwest Saskatchewan. Parks Canada then released 71 more into Saskatchewan's adjacent Grasslands National Park in 2005.[26]

Also surviving as potential bison habitat is Alberta's grassy Milk/Sage borderland, visited earlier in our journey. A Canada/U.S. prairie coalition (see page 170) has pinpointed the 10 best candidate areas for restoring fully functioning prairie ecosystems, and this borderland is the only one in Alberta. But the Alberta government rejects the idea, and the federal government turned down COSEWIC's recommendation to list the plains bison as a threatened species, even though it obviously is. Could

ABOVE AND FACING PAGE: *The Richardson's ground squirrel, bison, and grass evolved together. Today the bison are gone, leaving squirrels as the grassland's remaining keystone species: they provide food for numerous mammals and raptors, while their burrows are used by mammals, snakes, spiders, and owls.*

reintroduction work here, in southern Alberta? Nature's bison-grass association was so surpassingly productive, and the bison, unlike our water-dependent cattle, so adapted to droughty landscape, that the possibility is at least worthy of exploration.[27]

So there you are. This journey opened our eyes to the grasslands. What remarkable plants and animals remain, and how intricately interconnected – with one another, the landscape, and the prairie climate. What harm has been done over the years, and how rapid has been the decline of so many species in just the past two decades.

Hope is emerging, however. A deeper understanding of the land and our place in it is starting to take root among scientists, landowners, regional water users, and some urbanites and politicians – although far too few economists and business leaders. And the Fourth Assessment Report of the Intergovernmental Panel on Climate Change, issued in February 2007, jolted citizens and governments worldwide into a broad awareness and concern about climate and related issues – of special significance for semi-arid grasslands.

Nature has a demonstrated ability to produce seasonal abundance and winter sustenance out on the windswept prairie – one of the most endangered and least protected of all Canada's natural regions. Plants, animals – ourselves included, indeed whole landscapes will benefit if, instead of abusing Nature, we come to understand that we are part of Nature – that we are subject to her rhythms and laws and limits – and we go with the flow.

LEFT: *Black-crowned night herons were first seen in Alberta in 1958, at Strathmore. They nest in a few colonies at large waterbodies: in cattail islands in prairie sloughs and in willow trees in the parkland.*

FACING PAGE: *Dinosaur Provincial Park.*

Parks Are for People – and Wildlife. Or Are They?

In 1992, Canada was the first country to sign the *United Nations Convention on Biological Diversity,* by which it committed to establish a network of protected areas and enact and enforce law to protect endangered species. But our enthusiasm was short-lived. Today only about 10 percent of Canada is "protected." About 60 other nations do better.[28]

National parks encompass about 8 percent of Alberta and provide plants and animals more protection from industrial activity than virtually any other land in Canada. Furthermore, their boundaries are relatively secure, for they can be changed only by Act of Parliament. Nonetheless, visitors to Banff are often shocked, and many disgusted, at the extraordinary amount of development compared to national parks in other countries. And not just tourist development. In 1992 it took a lawsuit brought by environmental groups to stop clear-cut logging in Wood Buffalo National Park.[29]

Alberta's provincial parks are another story. Government claims that about 4 percent of Alberta lies within provincially protected lands. But many of these afford plants and animals little or no legal protection from industrial or intensive recreational activity. Indeed, provincial parks can be reduced or even eliminated by regulation "at the stroke of a politician's pen," without parliamentary process or public notice.[30]

Alberta has a confusing mishmash of protected lands, with names such as Heritage Rangeland, Wildland Park, Provincial Park, and Natural Area that imply protection but don't necessarily deliver. Why not? It's because the enabling law gives the minister broad discretion over the uses allowed in them. For example, the minister may either allow or prohibit activities such as oil and gas extraction, mining, hunting, off-highway vehicle use, and skiing in a provincial park.[31]

> *"I would feel more optimistic about a bright future for man if he spent less time proving that he can outwit Nature and more time tasting her sweetness and respecting her seniority."*
>
> E. B. WHITE (1899-1985), AMERICAN ESSAYIST

THE PARKLAND

Heartland Home

Marian White

IT'S SNOWING OUTSIDE and we're winter camping in Waterton. Right now, we're ensconced in the cozy lounge of the Kilmory Lodge. We've bagged a table by the log fire and are mulling over our plan for exploring the Parkland Natural Region.

When I think about it, parkland is where I feel most at home. Aspen parkland is unique to Canada's Prairie Provinces and just a little south into the U.S. From Minnesota, it arcs north around the grasslands, then down their western edge along the Rocky Mountain front. Being warmer than boreal forest and moister than coniferous forest or grassland, it favours deciduous trees. The Waterton area is the front line, a transition where aspen and fescue duke it out for supremacy over a fire-prone zone. Plants and animals from surrounding subregions mingle here, so its biodiversity ranks among the continent's richest. There's excitement in that edginess. Open exposures contain both threat and possibility, while trees and their shrub understoreys offer warmth and shelter – and the fear of lurking danger. That thrill must be as old as our kind, which evolved on the African savannah. It is a high for me.[1]

FACING PAGE: *The beautiful Rumsey landscape is extremely rare. Fescue and needle-and-thread grass cover the hillocks, and aspen groves full of birdsong and violets in early summer decorate the slopes. Wildflowers carpet flatter areas where badgers burrow, while chorus frogs, moose, and willows inhabit the marshy bottoms.*

79

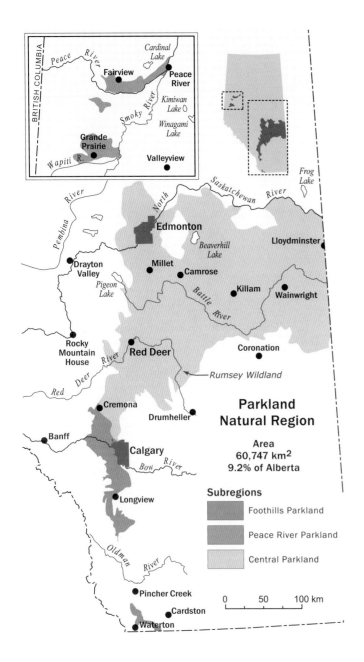

Parkland Natural Region

Area
60,747 km²
9.2% of Alberta

Subregions

Foothills Parkland

Peace River Parkland

Central Parkland

We sip our ale and refine our plan for the three subregions. It begins here and now in Waterton, in the Foothills Parkland. We'll explore it northward to Twin Butte, and from the Porcupine Hills to its far end at Cremona, north of Calgary, initially through short trips from home.

Late spring will find us in the Peace River Parkland, and summer, the Central Parkland. From Edmonton we'll meander to Wainwright and then return home in September south through Battle River country.

"Time to go," says Robin. We scoop up our clutter, pay our tab, and head back out into the snow. No one else is at the Pass Creek winter campsite. We push up *Song Dog*'s camper roof, fluff up our sleeping bags, crawl in, and are soon asleep in the silence of the winter night.

"'THE BUFFALO STILL VERY NUMEROUS ... running ... like waves in the sea.' What do you think of that, Mr. Bison?" I ask the bull bedded down in the snow, chewing his cud. He regards me through the mesh fence with a baleful eye.

It's morning. Robin and I have skied down the track to the bison's winter paddock near the trees at the edge of Waterton Park. The passage I'm quoting from was written in 1792-93 by surveyor Peter Fidler, the first explorer to observe and write in detail about Alberta's prairie and parkland.[2]

These were the domain of Blackfoot nomads whose economy and society depended on bison. In spring and summer, beast and Blackfoot spread far out on the prairie seeking fresh grass and good hunting. Come late autumn, the biting cold of the plains would drive them back west or north to the patchwork of tree cover and nutritious rough fescue. The Parkland was their winter home[3]

FACING PAGE: *It's spring. A mountain bluebird brings nesting material to a woodpecker hole in a cottonwood tree near Waterton. A mountain nester in the U.S., in Alberta it is common in the Montane Subregion and Parkland. It has recovered from low numbers early last century, due mainly to dedicated volunteers who have established and maintained bluebird nesting boxes on fence posts since 1971.*[4]

ABOVE: *Trumpeter swans chaperone young on migration north to breeding grounds in Alberta, the Northwest Territories, northeastern British Columbia, and the Yukon.*

FACING PAGE: *Trumpeter swans leave their wintering grounds west of Yellowstone in February. Mid-March finds the migrants resting on half-frozen ponds in the parkland and montane areas around Waterton. A growing flock of about 30 will stay in this vicinity to nest.*

"TRUMPETER SWANS ARE BACK!" It's mid-March when a friend calls from Waterton. Soon we're driving south, scouting for the returning migrants on ponds still largely covered with ice. I'm passionate about the swans, for they are, in a word, magnificent.

The narrow Foothills Parkland Subregion is the swans' migration corridor. It remains the most natural of the three parkland subregions. The southern portion's climate and terrain vary wonderfully over short distances, the prettiest country anywhere – like pictures in a children's book. Here, a mix of lupines, oat grasses, and fescue yields to groves of aspen and creeks with thickets of willow; then slopes clad in closed aspen forest, the mountains a stone's throw away.

But rangeland near Waterton is being converted to country-estate lots. This jacks up land prices beyond the reach of ranchers and tempts owners to sell out to developers. So ranchlands are dwindling, and with them the vital habitat they afford wildlife.

An example is the "Watertongate" affair. In 2001, Cardston County council ignored overwhelming public opinion and the objections of its neighbours – Parks Canada and the County of Pincher Creek, and approved a precedent-setting country residential subdivision on the park boundary. Such behaviour is "a recipe for conflict," said Craig Smith, courageous leader of the Prairie Crocus Ranching Coalition, which rallied to defend the ranchland.[5]

It's easy to fault the local council: landowners have a "God-given right to do what they want to do with the land," said one member of council. "Sometimes I wish wildlife would just go away," said another. But the real problem lies with the provincial government: to save money, it abandoned rural Albertans by scrapping its effective regional planning program.[6]

FOLLOWING PAGES: *Two cob (male) trumpeter swans engage in a territorial dispute while their mates look on. Trumpeters are the world's largest, rarest swans and unique to North America. Recovering from near extinction, in Alberta they migrate through the foothills subregions and nest largely in the Peace Parkland and neighbouring areas.*

A MONTH LATER WE AND THE SWANS ARE IN IAN TYSON COUNTRY from the Porcupine Hills up to Longview, but we're not the only arrivals. The latest groups attracted here and to the Central Parkland see not vital watersheds, good soils, wildlife habitat, cultural landscapes, or sheer beauty, but the opportunity for short-term gain from hydrocarbon production.

Alberta has exported so much oil and gas to the U.S. that our conventional oil production peaked in 1973 and natural gas in 2001. Despite small new finds, our marketable reserves are in desperate decline. A prudent government would aim to conserve this precious, non-renewable resource but instead, to stave off the looming gas shortage, ours is boosting rapid development of unconventional "tight" (hard-to-get-at) gas, and coalbed methane (CBM). These can have a huge footprint, requiring far more wells per section (one square mile) than does conventional oil and gas; so bad, the industry calls it "carpet-bombing."[7]

In 2005, journalist Andrew Nikiforuk reported that the density of such wells in the Rumsey Natural Area (Central Parkland) could reach 32 per section. In places similar to the Porcupine Hills/Livingstone area, it has reached 64. Each well and related infrastructure can disturb, on average, almost three acres, not counting attendant access roads and seismic lines. In Montana, wells have also contaminated or depleted surface waters and freshwater aquifers, and could here, too.[8]

Alberta landowners haven't taken this lying down. Ranchers on horseback from the Pekisko, Livingstone, and other groups rallied in protest in June 2005 in downtown Calgary in front of the Energy and Utilities Board office, demanding a moratorium on drilling. But they were ignored. There's no moratorium, well densities are increasing, and drilling continues.[9]

Excessive drilling would devastate Alberta's dwindling fescue grasslands. "Once destroyed, they are gone forever," says ecologist Cheryl Bradley. Cliff Wallis agrees: "Foothills Parkland south of Calgary is world-class aspen parkland. In a landscape so rare and beautiful, even one well is too many." Urban folk need to wake up to the vital link between protecting rural land

Two days ago on Broadcast Hill, Sunny and I walked knee-deep among wildflowers. Later, she put some in a vase and painted a picture of them, then flew home to England. This morning, a Sunday, I returned to that gorgeous wild hill – and found it ripped apart to create Calgary's Olympic Media Village. A big yellow machine sat there and from its maw hung a dying wild rose.

MARIAN'S DIARY, MID-JUNE 1987

FACING PAGE: *Country-estate subdivisions are gobbling up Foothills Parkland west of Calgary (downtown Calgary is at top, right), as well as farm- and ranchland all along the Rockies' Eastern Slopes.*

and water resources, and being able to put healthy food on the table. Urban support is urgently needed. Ranchers can't fight this alone.[10]

WE'RE AT THE WESTERN EDGE OF CALGARY NOW, in parkland south of the Trans-Canada Highway. For two decades, my back-road running routes crisscrossed its aspen bluffs and grazing lands beyond our Coach Hill home at what was, until recently, the city limit. I turn to my old field notes:

The prairie crocus, or pasque flower, is a harbinger of spring, one of the first flowers to push up through the snow on sunny hillsides and in fescue grasslands and dry, open woodlands.

> *Each year, I watch the seasons unfold run by run: ground squirrels emerging in March; then in April, prairie crocuses – and mountain bluebirds reclaiming nest-boxes on fence posts. Frogs are chorusing and catkins scent the air.*
>
> *May pulses with life: mule deer and whitetails graze pastures fringed by golden bean. Red-winged blackbirds, meadowlarks, and ruffed grouse proclaim their territories; and duck eggs hatch. June is ablaze with wild rose, prairie smoke, and lupine. Killdeer chaperone broods sporting black-and-white racing stripes. The pungent scent of wolf willow catches the breeze.*
>
> *Summer turns quiet. I swish my hands through foxtail barley as I run by. I catch sight of western wood lilies, or stop to stroke a horse's muzzle. Late August has an autumn nip to it. Bird families feast greedily on grass seed, and a weasel dashes across the road in search of prey.*
>
> *September brings rosehips and berries, frost, and autumn colours. Gathering flocks of birds turn noisy and rambunctious. There's expectancy in the air: Soon, flocks will lift in unison and migrate south.*
>
> *Five white-tailed deer, motionless in the deepening snow and cold, watch me on a winter run at sundown. They must think I'm crazy! Winter animals have minimalist energy budgets to last them through 'til spring.*

Rereading this breaks my heart. Urban sprawl and "starter-mansion" subdivisions have eaten up the landscape. My notes are all that remain of the wild communities along those no-longer-country roads.

"STOP! WHERE'S CHUI?" WE'RE BACKING DOWN THE DRIVE AGAIN, leaving home for the Peace River Parkland. Neighbours will feed our cat while we're away, and he has access to the outdoors. But I jump out of the truck and make sure he is not shut in the basement. Then we're off again.

A day's drive brings us to Saskatoon Island Provincial Park, 20 kilometres west of Grande Prairie. We camp. It's late April, when winter alternates with spring. The next day is chilly, overcast, and muddy underfoot. Wind drives horizontally through leafless aspens and lashes the grey lake, whipping up whitecaps. Bundled in down jackets at the end of the boat dock, we strain to see if the swans are out there in the gloom.

Trumpeters are unique to North America. Their near-extinction due to habitat loss and commercial hunting, and recovery due to a continuing hunting ban and heroic conservation efforts are remarkable. By 1932 a few persisted west of the Rockies. U.S. wildlife officials found only 69, all in western Yellowstone. But a small flock survived near Grande Prairie. It gradually expanded and spawned others, especially in the Yukon, but also southeast into parkland and adjacent areas. These Canadian swans overwinter with their cousins in Yellowstone.[11]

Robin and I spend days scouting Peace Parkland lakes for the swans, recording their numbers and behaviour. We chat with Dave Forseth, who farms by a trumpeter lake and appreciates the swans. "Their comings and goings mark the seasons," he says. Last autumn we had stood in his farmyard, watching cygnets taking flying lessons. A few miles away, farmer Danny Somerville enjoys having the swans around, too. The lake by his house is like an airport, noisy with arrivals and departures of trumpeters and other waterfowl.

Trumpeters now total around 35,000 but in Alberta remain threatened, numbering just over 1,000, with only 200 breeding pairs. Yet in 1998 the County of Grande Prairie tossed from its bylaws guaranteed 200-metre setbacks that had long protected the region's trumpeter lakes, substituting political discretion instead. In 2006 a provincial trumpeter recovery plan

Western wood lilies bloom in the parkland in July. But habitat loss and picking have greatly reduced their numbers. Picking removes the leaves – the plant's energy factory – along with the blossom. So enjoy it, but please don't pick this gorgeous flower.

was approved and work begun to implement it. Yet critical trumpeter habitat continues to be destroyed.[12]

THE DESIRABILITY of Alberta's Parkland has been its undoing. Moisture and deep, rich black soils made it the best natural region for agriculture. Today, relict parkland survives only on soils too poor or steep to plough, no longer representative of the original closed-canopy aspen forest. Farmers fleeing southern drought settled the Peace Parkland following the Dirty Thirties, and cleared and drained the land. Then came the 1970s oil and gas boom, bringing rapid population and industrial growth. So the Peace has become the most fragmented parkland of all. More than 99 percent of its native grassland is gone, along with 70 percent of its smaller wetlands.[13]

MID-MAY FINDS US JUST WEST OF EDMONTON in the Central Parkland. We're in a group led by wildlife biologist Lisa Takats Priestley in a gravelly, treed area, watching red-sided garter snakes mating.

"They're just emerging from their hibernaculum," she says. "About 9,700 overwintered here." She hands out surgical gloves so we can touch the snakes without harming them. A squatting dad introduces his toddler to the snakes, and three teenage girls overcome their fears and dare to pick up handfuls of the critters.

The species is in decline, Priestley tells us. "Many dens have been damaged or destroyed by dynamite, oil, fire and bulldozers," confirms a government report.

After our group leaves, we stay on with other visitors to take more pictures. I'm shocked to see a boy ride over some snakes with his bike, killing them. His parents fail to stop him or take the time to teach him to respect Nature. So I intervene and explain the Golden Rule – do as you would be done by. The boy then rides further off, away from the snakes. There is wisdom in the African proverb: it takes a village to raise a child.[14]

ABOVE: *Cool! Julie Pierce examines a red-sided garter snake while on an Edmonton Nature Club hike to a hibernaculum. Generally, it is a bad idea to crowd or handle wildlife, but this trip took place under the watchful eye of a professional biologist. Such trips are a great way to learn about Nature.*

FACING PAGE: *Red-sided garter snakes in a mating ball. In spring, males exit first from the hibernaculum and mate with females as they emerge. Hibernacula are protected under Alberta law, but not the snakes' other critical habitat.*

Beaverhill Lake was a major staging lake (used for resting) for vast flocks of white-fronted and snow geese migrating to and from their Arctic breeding grounds. Today, the lake is grass. We saw this flock of snow geese further south early one morning, on farmland near Camrose.

As we roll east to camp at Millet, I think of the snakes. Recently, our government designated their hibernacula as protected year round. Needed now are many more caring landowners, along with thoughtful dads and moms, and inquisitive teenagers reconnecting with Nature.

THE CENTRAL PARKLAND IS ALBERTA'S AGRICULTURAL HEARTLAND. Excellent farming conditions led to settlements, which in turn attracted more people. We're winding south through its broad Calgary-Edmonton corridor, home to 75 percent of Albertans. Pressures here are immense: agricultural, industrial, and urban growth has swallowed 90 percent of the Central Parkland's native habitat.

Lake and wetland country here and elsewhere in Canada's parkland and grassland is vital, representing more than half the continent's Prairie Pothole Region – the "Duck Factory" of North America. Yet the endangered piping plover has been allowed to be all but wiped out from its Central Parkland home, due mainly to recreational use of its nesting beaches.[15]

In June we're near Stettler, southeast of Red Deer at the Rumsey Natural Area. At 149 square kilometres, Rumsey is the world's largest surviving expanse of aspen parkland. Cheryl Bradley and naturalist Dorothy Dickson are leading a nature hike through this knob-and-kettle landscape, mostly Crown land. Today, Rumsey represents a type of landscape that's almost extinct.[16]

"Grazing leaseholders have been good stewards here for a hundred years," says watchdog Dickson. Then in 1996, our government granted Rumsey "protection" under its Special Places 2000 program. Yet, true to form, in 2002 and 2007 it allowed coalbed methane drilling here. In Alberta, the word "protected" is deceiving (see page 77).[17]

DROUGHT RETURNED TO THE CENTRAL PARKLAND in the new millennium. That becomes plain as we double back north to Beaverhill Lake: the 150-square-kilometre "lake" is now grass.[18]

Once it was famous for nesting birds, vast, migrating flocks, and nearby Tofield's annual Snow Goose Festival, Canada's largest birding event. The lake shrank and expanded several times before but in 2004 vanished almost completely and the festival along with it. It seems that human activities are taking their toll, says naturalist Dick Dekker. Lakewater goes to fill farmers' dugouts, flood hayfields, water cattle, and create wetland for ducks. Water expert Dr. David Schindler says industrial and residential wells likely have lowered the water table, drawing down the lake. So, along with $2 million a year in tourism revenue, Dekker says "the lake just blew away."[19]

It is 2002, a severe drought year, as we join a subdued crowd in blue jeans and Stetsons or baseball caps, in August, watching the Hay West train pull into Killam. The railcars are full of hay donated by easterners for central Alberta's desperate livestock owners. Vermilion farmer Byron Hart tells us local water wells, once 25 metres deep, now have to be drilled 70, even 150 metres deep, the water table has fallen so far.[20]

That's not surprising, given southern Alberta's long history of cyclical drought compounded, today, by climate change. The data point to summers averaging 2 to 4°C hotter globally by 2050, winters up 3 to 5°C, and weather events of greater intensity, including drought. A Killam woman says:

"It's dreadful, the farmers ripping out the hedges and trees to make bigger fields. We need the trees to make the rain." She's right, at one level. Of all the farmers we listen to, none makes the big-picture connection between the human contribution to global climate change and the devastation it is heaping upon farmers. But she comes the closest.[21]

After attending an auction of cattle that farmers can no longer feed, Robin and I head for home via Battle River country, past dried-up watercourses and sloughs, through a parched land turned to dust. We stop here and there to chat with local people and examine the land.

"A strong wind would blow that soil away," I say to a farmer's wife.

"Oh yes," she replies, "there's been a lot of that this year."

The rains will return. But likely so will even worse drought.[22]

ABOVE: *Climate change is a serious threat to agriculture, causing bouts of extreme weather, not just warmer temperatures. We photographed these scenes in the summer of 2002, just a few weeks apart.*
TOP: *Marian near Hughenden, south of Wainwright. Drought and overgrazing turned this cropland to dust.*
BOTTOM: *Flooded fields near Foremost, Alberta, in Alberta's Grassland Natural Region.*

*"The idea of wilderness needs
no defence, it only needs defenders."*

EDWARD ABBEY (1927-1989), AUTHOR,
OUTSPOKEN ENVIRONMENTALIST

THE FOOTHILLS

Wellspring of Life

Robin White

THIS IS AN AWFUL PLACE to break an ankle, I'm thinking, as I throw off my pack and leap into the river. Marian is thrashing about among some large boulders in waist-deep, cold, rushing water, struggling to get free from her 22-kilogram pack. For two hours we had boulder-hopped back and forth across the Littlehorn River before our luck ran out. Poised on a boulder midstream, she had carefully judged the distance and then leapt onto what appeared to be a large, dry, stable rock. Well, large and dry it was, but stable it wasn't. It rolled the instant she landed. As she fought to regain her balance, one of her adjustable hiking poles collapsed, sending her tumbling into the river.

Fortunately she escaped with just a few scrapes and bruises, and now that she has changed into dry clothes we're able to make light of it.

"Didn't you notice that was a providence rock?" I ask, and she smiles at our private joke. That's what we call rocks that move unexpectedly when you step on them. Why? Well, the famous 18th-century philosopher, poet, playwright and, we like to think, hardcore backpacker Wolfgang Goethe

FACING PAGE: *Marian fords the Blackstone River in the Upper Foothills, on the last day of our Bighorn backpacking trip.*

95

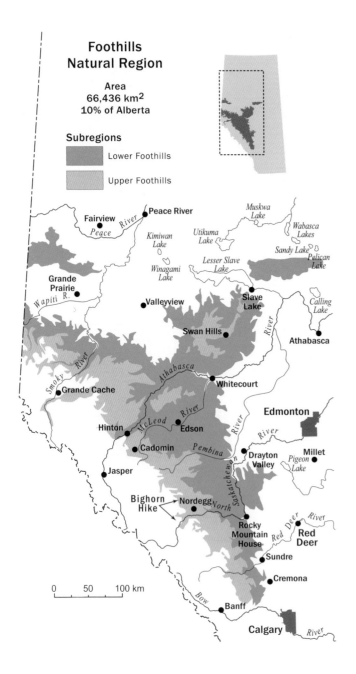

Foothills
Natural Region

Area
66,436 km²
10% of Alberta

Subregions

Lower Foothills

Upper Foothills

Muskwa Lake

Fairview

Peace River

Peace River

Kimiwan Lake

Utikuma Lake

Wabasca Lakes

Sandy Lake

Pelican Lake

Winagami Lake

Lesser Slave Lake

Grande Prairie

Wapiti R.

Valleyview

Slave Lake

Calling Lake

Smoky River

Swan Hills

Athabasca

Athabasca River

Grande Cache

Whitecourt

Edmonton

Hinton

McLeod River

Edson

River

River

Cadomin

Pembina

Millet

Pigeon Lake

Jasper

Drayton Valley

Saskatchewan

Bighorn Hike

Nordegg

North

Rocky Mountain House

Red Deer River

Red Deer

Sundre

Cremona

Bow

Banff

Calgary

River

0   50   100 km

---

once said, as he exhorted ditherers to stop dithering and act, "The moment that one commits oneself, then providence moves, too."

But it wouldn't have been a joke if she'd broken an ankle, so no more playing Russian roulette with providence rocks. From here on, we take our boots off and wade the rivers, regardless of the extra time it takes. We can't afford a serious accident, for we are three days into a six-day hiking trip through the Bighorn Wildland, a fabulous part of the Foothills Natural Region.

Many people regard the Bighorn as horse country, but I'm not a horse person. In 1966, while on a mountaineering expedition, I rode a bony mountain pony – with just a folded piece of sack cloth for a saddle and no stirrups – for ten days through the rugged Hindu Kush Mountains of Afghanistan. Now, whenever I see a horse, I instinctively wince as I relive the pummelling my backside received.

The Bighorn may be well suited to horses, but it is also great hiking country for anyone looking for the sort of wilderness experience you are unlikely to find on the more popular trails of the national parks. In the Bighorn you won't find signposts or crowded campsites – or handrails. Hikers must be self-sufficient, know how to read a map, and be prepared for any emergency.

WE HAD SET OUT from the David Thompson Highway with the goal of reaching the trailhead at Blackstone River, north of Nordegg, about 100 kilometres away. Late July is the ideal time for hiking the foothills, and we had spent the first two days moving at a leisurely pace up Whitegoat Creek to Littlehorn Pass and on to Bighorn Pass. Friends said we'd see lots of wildflowers and we've not been disappointed. The trail started in mixed forest carpeted in western wood lilies, red Indian paintbrush, larkspur, pale yellow columbine, and many other wildflowers. Below Bighorn Pass we had

FACING PAGE: *Lower Foothills old-growth forest on Marten Mountain by Lesser Slave Lake. More tree species are found in this subregion than anywhere else in Alberta.*

stopped in a beautiful meadow where a family of marmots scurried about among the rocks, while in the valley below, the Littlehorn River gurgled and tumbled over two picturesque waterfalls.

What a place. It would have been easy to abandon our hike and stay there until our food ran out. But we didn't. We needed to explore some more. The next day we had followed the river downstream until we lost the trail on a broad shingle bar. At that point, we had embarked on the series of hazardous river crossings that just led to Marian's impromptu bath.

It's day three. We reach Bighorn Meadows and linger waist high in violet-blue delphiniums, a gorgeous native plant, and golden buttercups, equally gorgeous but possibly the tall buttercup – an introduced noxious weed toxic to grazing animals. A cutline leads north into forest where, at the top of a hill, a new horse trail cuts west through the trees. We ponder whether or not to follow it, but we decide to play it safe and stick to the main trail, which we know will take us to Sunkay Meadows and eventually Sunkay Lake.

Whoever gave Sunkay Meadows its appealing name either has never been there or has a twisted sense of humour. Mapmakers should rename it "Stay-away Bog!" To my mind, much of it isn't meadow at all; it's muskeg swamp that could swallow a horse. For three hours we slosh along its western edge with our heavy packs and soaking wet boots. When the map shows our trail continuing on the far side of the valley, we cross over by leaping from one table-sized shrub mound to the next, cursing whenever a foot slips, threatening to send us plunging into the seemingly bottomless wells of black water.

Crossing a creek on a beaver dam, we at last find an animal trail leading uphill and out of the swamp's clutches. A few kilometres more and we're on an old cart track that is easy to follow but frequently blocked by deadfall. Eventually the trail improves, and with just enough daylight left to pitch camp, we arrive weary and a little sore at Sunkay Lake. As the sun goes down, our only company is a common loon. We fall asleep to its haunting call – the quintessential sound of the Canadian wild.

ABOVE: *Porcupines live a solitary life in North American forests and even on the plains, browsing bark, twigs, and leaves of coniferous and deciduous trees. Their 30,000 or so barbed quills protect them by lodging in the flesh of attackers, causing pain and even death.*

FACING PAGE: *Robin was setting up his blind in aspen woodland when this cock ruffed grouse mounted a rock nearby and began drumming at regular intervals to attract a mate. The low-frequency sound – like a two-stroke motorbike engine struggling to start on a cold day – is made by the compression of air as the grouse beats its wings, slowly at first, then so fast they become a blur.*

*Perched above George Creek
near journey's end, I ask: was
it worth the effort, the thirst,
blisters, and aching limbs?*

*You bet it was - for the
discovery of a landscape new
to us, the tranquility, free of
care, out in Nature. We need
this tonic to stay sane and
nurture our souls.*

MARIAN'S DIARY, 30 JULY 2003

Early next morning, we reach a beautiful, sparkling creek, the Wapiabi, its shingle bars pink with flowers. The trail continues on the far side, so we put on our runners and splash across, relishing the gentle foot massage the cold water provides. After eight more crossings, the trail leads us away from the creek, through its broad, open valley dotted with aspen stands and a profusion of wildflowers.

Around midday a horse whinnies, and moments later we come upon several horses grazing in a temporary enclosure created by a single-strand electric fence. Nearby, eight people are relaxing in a camp among the aspen, ringed by three large, outfitter's tents.

"Come on over and have a coffee," calls out a wiry man with tufts of grey hair sprouting out from under a broad-brimmed cowboy hat. "Where are you headed?"

Glad of a break we hike over, put down our packs, and find logs to sit on. Several men gather around. A plump, matronly woman places a coffee pot on the metal grill over a fire flaring up from a huge ring of stones. They tell us they've seen no other hikers in the 10 days they've been camped at this spot. And, yes, that new trail we passed on the hill before "Stay-away Bog" was indeed the correct one, and would have spared us the tough slogging that followed.

The depth of this group's love of wild Alberta is impressive. Here are three generations of farmers and ranchers who take two weeks off work every summer to hold a family get-together at this spot. You might expect that, after working their farms all year, any break they get would be spent lolling on a beach in Mexico sipping piña coladas. Not so, these folks! They take their horses and camp in the Bighorn.

Eventually bidding the family farewell, we head off along the trail, which soon leads down again to Wapiabi Creek. In a while, it turns up a grassy valley speckled with wildflowers and flanked by low, forested hills. One could easily while away a week or a month exploring here.

It's mid-afternoon as we descend to some shrubby flats called Indian

Graves and make a final crossing of the Wapiabi. Some tricky navigation keeps us on course, zigzagging up through river terraces, forest, side valleys, and 50-year-old cutlines that show remarkably little sign of healing. At dusk we emerge, hot and thirsty, from the forest at the rim of a broad, grassy basin with a small stream running through it: upper George Creek. Scouting around, we find an outfitter's camp among pines with an excellent view of the basin eastward and Front Ranges to the west.

We've seen surprisingly little wildlife on this trip so far but, while brewing tea at six the next morning, we hear horses neighing. An approaching pack train? No. Seven dark brown, feral horses have come to drink at the creek. Then they offer up a few snorts and canter back across the basin, into the forest. Feral horses have run wild in the foothills for 200 years, but only 191 were found in the government's 2006 aerial count. We are lucky to have seen this herd.

Packing up our dew-drenched tent, we hit the trail in heavy mist. The route from here is unclear but despite a couple of blisters, we are energized by yesterday's wonderful hiking in the Wapiabi valley. An ankle-wrenching horse trail winds through forest, leading us onto a boggy willow plateau just as the sun pokes through and starts burning off the mist. Then the trail diagonals down to a lively creek, which leads eventually to the broad lower George Creek valley.

A well-used horse trail along the valley bottom takes us at length to the confluence with the Blackstone River. Fording it, we turn sharp east and enter the impressive gorge of Blackstone Gap. A narrow trail across a talus slope above the churning, boulder-filled river sees us through the gorge and into forest again. There we find the trailhead and our camper parked under some trees where we had left it six days earlier. It has been a fabulous trip and, apart from the horse party, we feel we had the Bighorn all to ourselves.

WILL HIKING THE BIGHORN be as memorable for future generations? Likely not, and here's why. It has long been recognized that the Eastern

Marian catches up on her field notes on a hillside overlooking the lower George Creek valley.

ABOVE: *Next to people, beaver are the biggest animal shapers of the landscape. Their sturdy dams create the extensive ponds and lakes they need, which also prove valuable wetland habitat for many other species, from moose and weasels to birds and fish.*

FACING PAGE: *A beaver hauls mud onto its lodge. A family builds its lodge on an island or stick platform, then plasters it with mud. Underwater entrances make it difficult for any predator, other than an otter, to gain access. Roofs of thickly woven twigs, smeared with mud, freeze in late fall to become virtually impenetrable, even by black bears.*

Slopes region, meaning the Alberta side of the Rocky Mountains plus the foothills, is critically important to all the Prairie Provinces, not just Alberta: it is the watershed that provides them with reliable supplies of clean water.

So, the provincial government's Eastern Slopes Policy (1977) was created to afford some protection to the region. That, and its relative remoteness, kept the Bighorn largely free of development for 24 years. The policy designated most of the Bighorn as "prime protection," meaning off-limits to off-highway vehicles (OHVs) and resource extraction. Furthermore, the government signalled its intention to keep the area that way by publishing maps and brochures that referred to most of it as the "Bighorn Wildland Recreation Area." But that protection never progressed beyond policy which, unlike law, can be changed with little or no public scrutiny.

And that's what happened. In 2001, with the sharp rise in oil and natural gas prices, the pressure for drilling in the foothills increased dramatically. With minimum public consultation, the government declared the Bighorn Wildland no longer protected and stopped printing Bighorn Wildland Recreation Area maps. Instead, a motorized-recreation plan was prepared and new "Bighorn Backcountry" maps printed, indicating no protection from resource development. It then started issuing subsurface leases while allowing OHVs into areas where they were never allowed before.

The responsible use of OHVs is a legitimate recreational activity – but not everywhere. OHVs are controversial because they compact and erode soils, damage streams and hiking and equestrian trails, stress wildlife, facilitate illegal hunting, and cause noise and air pollution, diminishing the enjoyment of other backcountry users significantly.

Today the *Eastern Slopes Policy* is largely ignored by government. Trail riding, hiking, and hunting – uses generally compatible with watershed and wildlife habitat protection – continue as before in the Bighorn. But there's also logging and oil and gas exploration, which involve road building and tree removal that fragment the forest and are clearly incompatible with watershed protection.[1]

The Bighorn, of course, isn't the only area threatened by intensive resource development. There are many others. One such, way up north, is the Chinchaga Forest. We drive there, next, through the lush foothills.

THE CHINCHAGA FOREST (since deemed Boreal, see map, page 120) lies some 230 kilometres north of Grande Prairie. Helene Walsh, a feisty ecologist with the Canadian Parks and Wilderness Society (CPAWS), joins us in Fairview and we continue north to the Chinchaga Forestry Trunk Road turn-off with its jumble of oil and gas contractors' signs. The gravel road takes us west through 100 kilometres of gently rolling terrain, past an initial swath of grazing land to a succession of large clear-cuts, partially hidden from public view by a thin veneer of living trees. Some call these "public deception" belts.

Helene leads us to a superb stretch of old-growth forest along Halverson Ridge. It's a glorious place, the fall colours nearing their peak and groves of brilliant yellow aspens contrasting with dark green spruce. Squirrels race along branches, biting off cones to store in their middens for winter, and a flock of sandhill cranes call to one another as they fly overhead on their southerly migration.

This old-growth forest is a patchwork of trees of varying species, size, and age, providing shade and moist cover for horsetail, bunchberry, and a rich assortment of mushrooms. There are big, old, lichen-draped spruce trees with mossy bases; crimson-leaved wild currant ablaze with shiny red fruit; standing snags riddled with woodpecker holes; fallen trunks leaning against healthy ones, like drunken sailors; teenage pines reaching vigorously up to the light; and seedlings starting life on the moss-covered backs of rotting nurse logs. Two mule deer appear at the forest edge, but we see no lynx or wolves, although the Chinchaga is one of the best places to see them.

Helene explains that CPAWS, along with other conservation groups, has pushed unsuccessfully for many years for legal protection of the Chinchaga.

ABOVE AND FACING PAGE: *Sandhill cranes nest in secluded marshes and bogs, so are most easily seen when migrating. Due to settlement and farming, this most abundant of cranes no longer breeds in the grasslands. But they seem to be expanding their range south again from the boreal and foothills forest. Listen for their rattling call during migration. They winter in southern U.S. and Mexico.*

ABOVE: *Like much of the boreal and foothill regions, the Chinchaga Forest near Manning is crisscrossed by a spiderweb of industrial roads, pipe-, and power lines. They bar movement of woodland caribou and grizzly bears, which typically avoid coming within 100 metres of "roads," even little-used ones. And they provide easy access for OHVs and hunters, wolf and human, to such animals' once-remote havens.*

The density of these routes is "arguably the single most serious and detrimental consequence of industry in the foothills," says forest expert Dr. Richard Thomas.[2]

FACING PAGE: *It is September in mixedwood habitat. A cloud of spores ejects from puffball mushrooms as heavy rain strikes.*

FOLLOWING PAGES: *Shown from the air, the Chinchaga River meanders across terrain with little slope, seeking its way via the Hay and Mackenzie rivers to the Arctic Ocean. In times of flood, it may shortcut across the neck of a meander, leaving a remnant oxbow lake.*

Government and industry claim that ecologically sensitive techniques are being used to ensure that our forests are being managed sustainably and biodiversity maintained. CPAWS argues that, even if that were true, it would be prudent to first set aside large areas of natural forest to act as ecological benchmarks against which to measure the success or failure of the industry's techniques. According to the government's own report, the Chinchaga is "by far the best candidate" for such a benchmark. Helene would like to see a protected area of at least 5,500 square kilometres, which experts believe is sufficiently large not to be wiped out in one huge fire. So far the government's response falls far short: only 800 square kilometres has been protected, none from oil and gas activity, and Halverson Ridge not at all.[3]

We will spend a week exploring the Chinchaga, but Helene has to get back to Fairview. As she climbs into her car, she turns and says with a wry grin: "Enjoy this place now because in two or three years, the old forest on Halverson Ridge may have become Halverson Stumps!"

That's depressing. Too much old-growth has already been cut down in Alberta. And the Chinchaga is fragmented enough by logging and well sites, service roads, and pipe-, seismic and transmission lines. Woodland caribou survive by using remote old-growth forest, far from moose, elk, deer, and the wolves those prey attract. Corridors bulldozed into such territory render caribou unnaturally accessible to wolves and other predators, pushing them rapidly to extirpation. What to do?

In 2006, industry decided to capture, fence, and feed pregnant and lactating females and their newborns for a few months, like domestic livestock, to protect them from wolves. But the trial ended just months later when it was found to have increased, not decreased, wolf predation on the calves. The strategy addressed only symptoms of caribou decline, not the cause (habitat disturbance or loss). The same applies to the government's tactic: first shoot the wolves that prey on the caribou. Then, when moose and elk populations explode due to lack of wolves, shoot them as well. Brilliant! Soon we'll have the fragmented forest to ourselves.[4]

ALBERTA'S FORESTS: "SUSTAINABLE" UNTIL GONE

In the mid-1980s, oil prices collapsed and a desperate provincial government sought to diversify the economy and increase local employment. With 87 percent of the province's forest on public land, it ignored the needs of small local mills and brought in international logging companies by offering them huge subsidies and long-term cutting rights to some 20 percent of the province.[5]

Although the public clearly expects a balance between timber extraction and conservation, in practice, forests are still managed chiefly for economic return. About 90 percent of logging comprises the clear-cutting of virgin forest from land that is then replanted with a few commercial species, like an agricultural crop. Such plantations are logged every 70 years or so, well before a natural, complex forest with diverse flora and fauna has time to get re-established.[6]

Lumber is used in construction, but nearly half the cut is pulped, much going to the U.S. to make tissue paper and junk mail: most of the 17 billion catalogues mailed there each year are produced from new timber, not recycled paper. And most are thrown, unread, into the garbage.[7]

Forest is also cleared for farming and urban expansion, while the oil and gas industry cuts down (without paying any "stumpage" royalty and usually without replanting) almost as many trees as the loggers, for well sites, roads, seismic lines, and the like. Poor co-ordination between logging and energy interests results in much duplication of roading and unnecessary forest loss and damage. The cumulative effect shows: Alberta's forests are among the most fragmented in Canada.[8]

So what are the public benefits? Although large, automated pulp mills are capital, not labour intensive, logging still provides some 54,000 jobs in Alberta, which produce household income and tax revenue. But Alberta's timber royalties are set low (realizing only $130 million in 2004–05), and when you subtract government costs for road upgrades, forest administration, firefighting, and insect control, royalties alone may not even cover costs.[9]

There is hope, however, that Alberta will see more sensitive forest management. In 2005 Al-Pac, the biggest and one of the province's most progressive logging companies, received certification from the internationally recognized Forest Stewardship Council (FSC) for 5.5 million hectares. This is the largest expanse of FSC-certified forest in the world. Also, the Boreal Forest Initiative (see page 168) looks promising.

ABOVE, LEFT: *Forestry means selectively felling trees so the forest lives on. Alberta, on the other hand, mostly clear-cuts its forests and replaces them with tree plantations.*

LEFT, TOP: *Lacking legal protection, this mixed stand of old-growth aspen and conifers on Halverson Ridge in the Chinchaga Forest will likely end up as dimensional lumber or pulp.* BOTTOM: *"Keep cool," reads the box discarded by tree planters. But that isn't going to happen in a clear-cut, where sun and wind dry out exposed soils and logging waste – which fuels forest fires. Clear-cutting is the cheapest way to log, and conventional replanting creates stands of the same tree species, age, and size that make for good fibre flow – for a short while. But the resulting plantations are more prone to disease, insect damage, and fire and lack the wildlife habitat diversity of natural forest.*

The alternative, selective logging, is more labour intensive and costly but provides more local jobs, leaves the forest ecosystem intact and, done properly, ensures a healthy and productive – a genuine – future forest.[10]

BELOW: *Marian (left) and Helene Walsh enjoy the Chinchaga Forest, west of Manning.*

The Whitehorse Creek Wildland Park at the Cardinal Divide is deservedly popular among butterfly enthusiasts. ABOVE, TOP: *Northern marble butterfly.* BOTTOM: *Anicia checkerspot butterfly.*

FACING PAGE: *The landmark curve of the Cardinal Divide reaches up through foothills forest into the subalpine zone.*

THE CARDINAL DIVIDE IS A FAVOURITE PLACE OF OURS and we decide to stop there on our way home. Arriving at Hinton, we turn south down Highway 40 to the hamlet of Cadomin and pull in at the Hole-in-the-Wall – a gas station and popular restaurant. A pot of tea and a couple of slices of homemade pie put us in a mellow mood, and we chat about what lies ahead.

This part of the foothills is known as the Coal Branch. More than a dozen underground coal mines operated here in the early 1900s until the advent of the diesel locomotive, around 1950. Coal found here is the high-carbon kind used for iron-smelting and in much demand today, especially in Asia. But it's the uniqueness and beauty of the place, not coal, that's the attraction for most visitors.

We leave the Hole-in-the-Wall excited at the prospect of revisiting the Cardinal Divide, but as we approach Whitehorse Creek, our hearts sink. The old iron bridge is still there and so, too, the little road winding its way up the McLeod River valley; but they are now dwarfed by the massive, parallel earth berm and industrial haul road used to transport coal from the Cardinal River mine.[11]

The McLeod River below, which until recently was so picturesque, is now edged by an ugly power line. Memories surface of great times watching harlequin ducks busily seeking food in the McLeod's turbulent waters or basking on its rocks. They built their nests and raised their young along the river's small tributaries.

At the head of the valley, we reach an open, flatter landscape where headwater streams converge. Here are the greened-up remains of Mountain Park, a mining town that was once the highest settlement in Canada. Today the cemetery, but little else, survives, well cared for by the Mountain Park Environmental Protection & Heritage Association.

Beyond Mountain Park, the road is poorly maintained and steep, but stick with it and it will bring you to one of the great viewpoints of the Alberta foothills: the Cardinal Divide. From this part of the North

American continental divide, the McLeod and Cardinal headwaters flow, respectively, north to the Arctic Ocean and east to the Atlantic. To the southwest, beautiful open subalpine meadows provide the foreground to a breathtaking panorama of snow-capped mountains. An easy 30-minute hike up the obvious ridge to the northeast provides stunning views in all directions – all, that is, except to the north, where you look across at the first of the new coal mine's open pits gouged from the landscape.

The Cardinal Divide and what remains of the Mountain Park area's bottomlands make up a nationally important biological "hot spot." Wildlife includes some 29 species of birds and mammals listed as being rare or in trouble in Alberta, including grizzly bear, wolverine, bull trout, and Alberta's second-largest population of harlequin ducks.[12]

As for plants, the divide is reckoned to have been a refugium – a place not scoured by glaciers in the Wisconsin Ice Age. As a result, its surviving aquatic, insect, and plant life is varied and unusual. The Alberta Native Plant Council (ANPC) has recorded over 250 plant species there, including 15 that are provincially significant and 3 nationally so. But these plants depend for life on the microclimate afforded by the soil and rocks that surround them. Disturb this balance and it may be decades before the plants recover, if at all.[13]

And disturbed it has been. The old Mountain Park underground mines caused considerable local surface damage, and the townsite has become a

Canada's Atlantic harlequin duck population is listed as endangered, while its Pacific population, whose breeding range reaches east into Alberta's Rockies and Upper Foothills, is simply uncommon. Albertans are responsible for protecting the harlequins breeding in our province and the habitat they use.

LEFT, TOP: *The harlequin duck's name reflects the similarities of the drake's plumage to the colourful patchwork garb of Harlequin, traditional King of Pantomime.*

BOTTOM: *Harlequin hens and young seek invertebrate food in shallow, fast-flowing mountain and foothill forest streams. This hen nested in what was pristine habitat in the upper McLeod River drainage.*

staging area for OHVs that cause more-extensive damage. One summer we spent a weekend helping ANPC members, assisted by some 20 schoolchildren, trying to repair OHV tracks made in the divide's fragile soil. To prevent further erosion, we cut channels to drain water away from the threadbare tracks. Then we drilled holes and planted clumps of native grass. It was slow, laborious work. Miles of such tracks on the Cardinal Divide need repair, and all our party managed to do was make a start at reclaiming a short stretch. Still, we were glad to help, for we thought we were making a difference.

We were wrong. Now, as we drive on, and as a later flight over the area will confirm, this once beautiful landscape is being disfigured on a breathtaking scale.

THE CARDINAL RIVER MINE consists of a series of open pits, which, if all are developed, will stretch for 23 kilometres, a distance as wide as the city of Edmonton. For each tonne of coal extracted, roughly eight tonnes of rock, trees, soil, shrubs, and flowers – termed "overburden" by miners – is ripped up and dumped onto the surrounding landscape, filling valleys, burying streams, and destroying wildlife habitat and the aesthetic beauty of the Mountain Park area.

The mine project differs substantially from that first approved, which involved on-site coal-processing. Instead, up to 24 hours a day, seven days a week, monster trucks carry 220-tonne loads down the 22-kilometre haul road to be processed at the old Luscar mine.

Government and many Hinton companies support the mine. So coal production is proceeding despite the concerns of Environment Canada, Parks Canada, and the United Nations World Heritage Committee for the negative effects it will have on the critical habitat and movements of

RIGHT: *The Cardinal Divide is rich in wildflowers.*

115

grizzlies and other wildlife to and from Jasper National Park, less than three kilometres away; despite Canadian Wildlife Service predictions that it will likely cause the loss of 4,000 to 5,000 songbirds from the area, including 32 species already in decline in North America; despite the health risks to people and wildlife from selenium from the mine's contaminating water bodies; despite the loss of rare plants, harlequin duck breeding habitat, and trout-spawning streams; and despite the revised project's not having had an environmental impact assessment.[14]

Mining coal for steel-making is a boom-bust industry. When the Cardinal River mine closes, what of the future? The Sierra Club of Canada's Dianne Pachal speaks for many who love this area and know the importance of protecting what remains:

"Once Mountain Park is irreparably damaged, the grizzly bear and migratory-bird habitat gone, and the mine with its 120 jobs [not even the 420 promised] closed in 15 years or less, what then for Hinton and Cadomin? [Worldwide], mined-over landscapes are not a scarce commodity; but wildland parks, World Heritage Sites, and critical wildlife habitat are."[15]

FACING PAGE: *The Cardinal River (formerly Cheviot) coal mine, June 2005. The mine is the first in a proposed chain of open pits stretching 23 kilometres along the foothills on public land. These will be reclaimed but the land cannot be restored to its former condition.*

The Sonoran Institute, an economic research group, analyzed the success or failure of small communities along the Rocky Mountain front. It warns that dependency on boom-bust resource industries will not ensure long-term prosperity. The most successful communities have diverse economies close to the beautiful scenery of protected public lands that offer good recreational opportunities. So the Cheviot mine issue isn't about jobs versus the environment. It's about short-term jobs that destroy the environment versus long-term jobs that capitalize on a protected environment.

RIGHT: *Alberta Native Plant Council volunteers line a runoff diversion channel with rocks as part of an effort to restore the sensitive subalpine landscape of the Cardinal Divide, damaged by off-highway vehicles.*

THE BOREAL FOREST

Freeze-dried Zone

Robin White

"**S**URE YOU CAN DO IT. Just pretend you're early pioneers, get yourselves a canoe, and go for it," says Jumbo. "It's an easy trip. All you have to worry about is crossing Lake Athabasca. It can be treacherous in a wind. So, get to the lake really early in the morning, aim for the radio tower above Fort Chip, and paddle like hell!"

We're in the Twin Pines Motel in Fort McMurray, talking on the telephone with Jumbo Fraser, a trapper and well-respected guide in Fort Chipewyan, some 280 kilometres to the north. But pretending to be early pioneers isn't why we want to paddle the Athabasca and Slave rivers the 450 kilometres to Fort Fitzgerald, the takeout point for Fort Smith. We just want to experience these rivers and add to our knowledge of the Boreal Forest Natural Region and its wildlife.

Now, Marian and I aren't really boat people. True, back in England before we were married, in a failed attempt to impress, I had once rowed her around the Serpentine, a shallow, artificial lake in London's Hyde Park. But that was nearly 40 years ago and hardly sufficient preparation for

FACING PAGE: *The Salt Plains of Wood Buffalo National Park are unique. Islands of stunted spruce and bog-birch shrubs rise from a 200-square-kilometre expanse of salt-tolerant grass and other herbs. Devonian salt beds roughly 400 million years old lie just below the surface. In hot summers, salt cones, some a metre high and two wide, build at the foot of the scarp around springs up to 10 times saltier than seawater.*[1]

119

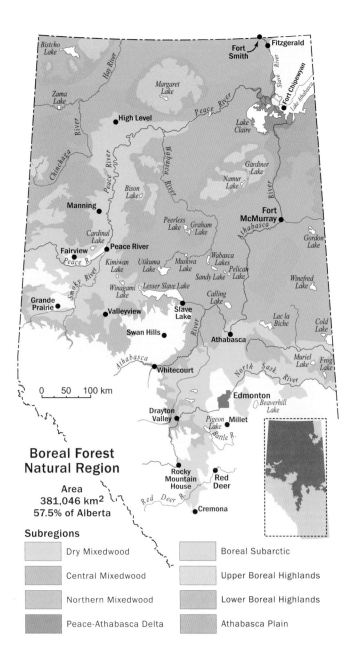

Boreal Forest Natural Region

Area
381,046 km²
57.5% of Alberta

Subregions

Dry Mixedwood	Boreal Subarctic
Central Mixedwood	Upper Boreal Highlands
Northern Mixedwood	Lower Boreal Highlands
Peace-Athabasca Delta	Athabasca Plain

tackling Alberta's great rivers. So we took a two-day paddling course on the Bow River and hired Brad Bourque, a Fort Smith outfitter who was licensed and recommended to us by Parks Canada, to guide our boreal adventure. But Bourque failed to show at the agreed meeting point in Fort McMurray. On calling his home to find out where he was, we were told he wouldn't be coming. What to do?

One option is to abandon the trip. But why, when we have our camping equipment, drybags, stove, two weeks' food, and lots of wilderness camping experience? Canoes and life jackets we can rent. We lack a satellite phone for emergencies but, hey, if Sir Alexander Mackenzie didn't bother with one when he paddled these rivers in 1792, they can't be essential. So we decide to go for it.

John Semple of Points North Adventures is helpful and encouraging. He rents us a double canoe – and Sandra Foss, who had also signed up with Bourque, a single canoe, which she pluckily insists only she will paddle. He also lends us a set of hydrographic charts covering our route.

The trip will be a challenge, for the rivers are huge, the area remote, and being September, few people will be around if we get into trouble. John says that, while many parties talk of doing so, only about half a dozen a year paddle all the way from Fort McMurray to Fort Fitzgerald.

NAVIGATING THE ATHABASCA RIVER is tricky. It is shallow and obstructed by shifting sandbars, and in places entire islands shown on the charts have been swept away. Our hydrographic charts identify most islands not by name but by type of vegetation. Usually this is "willow and poplar," "poplar and willow," or just plain "willow." So, as we pick our way through these

FACING PAGE: *Black bears are considerably smaller than grizzly and polar bears, but meet with more success. They need smaller home ranges, so are more numerous, and they produce more cubs more often than other bears. Also they can adapt to almost any food source and forest habitat.*

islands, we hold many ridiculous conversations more reminiscent of Monty Python than Sir Alexander Mackenzie. "There's an island dead ahead. Which way, right or left?"

"Well, if it's a willow and poplar island, the chart says we go left."

"No, I see only willow, but the island we passed five minutes ago, that had poplar."

"I don't think it did. All I saw was willow!"

"That's because you were fiddling with your camera. I definitely saw poplar. Hold on, there's another island coming into view and I think it has poplar as well as willow."

"Are you sure that you're looking at an island and not just at the far bank?"

"Of course I'm sure.... No wait ... yes, you're right.... It is the far bank!"

At which point there is a scraping sound and all forward motion stops. We have run up on a sandbar.

WE HOPE THAT THE REMOTENESS of the place and the silence of the canoes will reward us with some magical sightings of animals, and our second morning on the river provides just that. I crawl out of the tent at dawn and happen to glance upstream. The sun is just cresting the horizon and mist is rising off the river, a classic study for a watercolour artist. But that isn't all. Four black wolves are swimming across less than 100 metres away. We have a perfect view of them.

When the lead animal, likely the alpha male, climbs onto a gravel bar, he turns and looks at us. Deciding that we aren't a serious threat, he slips back into the water and continues swimming strongly toward the far shore. Now the other three wolves reach the gravel bar but are clearly more nervous. They look at their leader, then at us, and then back at the big male, trying to weigh up the potential threat. But they turn and swim back the way they have come. The alpha male reaches the far bank and scrambles up. He shakes himself, and spray, backlit by the sun, flies from his fur; then,

ABOVE: *Marian tows our canoe off a sandbar. In early September, the water in the Athabasca River is now so shallow that we are constantly searching for suitable channels, and running aground when we fail.*

FACING PAGE: *Historically, wolves were respected by natives but feared and persecuted by European settlers. Today, we understand the wolf's key role in maintaining ecosystem balance by holding in check the numbers of ungulates and medium-sized predators. This maintains healthy populations of willows, hence beaver and songbirds. Alberta's wolf population is estimated to fluctuate annually around 4,200 individuals, in packs of 9 or so animals plus 12 percent lone wolves.[2]*

ABOVE AND FACING PAGE: *Whooping cranes are severely endangered. Despite protected status, indiscriminate hunting and habitat disturbance drove them to near extinction. By 1941 only 16 remained, in a single wild flock. By autumn 2006, the flock numbered some 230 birds. It still migrates from Wood Buffalo National Park to winter on the Texas coast – where it is vulnerable to oil spills.*

A major restoration effort including captive breeding began in the 1970s and continues, including at Calgary Zoo. By mid-2006, whooping cranes numbered 470 – that's 336 wild and 134 captive.[3]

glancing over his shoulder at us, he ambles across to the trees and melts from sight. Likely the others will join him once we are gone.

Birdlife in the boreal forest is highly seasonal. In winter, resident species are few and include owls, woodpeckers, jays, finches, and chickadees. But in the spring, birds arrive by the millions from as far away as Central and South America. At least 300 species, from warblers and loons to the world's only remaining wild migratory flock of whooping cranes, arrive to breed and raise their young. But what make the boreal forest so special are the songbirds – the sparrows, thrushes, and warblers that brighten the countryside, our gardens, and our lives as they pass through on their way north. They come north to feed off the vast swarms of insects.[4]

Warblers are really tropical birds that spend less than four months here in furious activity, breeding and raising their families. By mid-August, their vivid breeding plumage is replaced by drab greys and browns. Then they, together with their offspring, head south again to overwinter. The warblers had mostly left before we started our journey, but we enjoy seeing plenty of other birds: kingfishers, bald eagles, sandpipers, lesser yellowlegs, boreal chickadees, northern flickers, white-crowned sparrows, sandhill cranes, and various woodpeckers.

FINDING CLEAN DRINKING WATER is always a problem on this canoe trip. Downstream from the Athabasca's pulp mills and tar sands, I fill a glass bottle from the river and find it so laced with tar deposits, noxious brown froth, and slime that it is almost opaque. So we fill our water containers exclusively from side streams and filter every drop.

Finding a place to camp is no easier, for the river banks are often steep or muddy, capped by thick forest with heavy underbrush. But sometimes we don't need a campsite. One morning a motor launch, ploughing upstream on the far side of the river, spies us and comes over. At the wheel is a jolly, middle-aged man with a big belly. "They call me Krazy George," he says, "and this is my friend Steve." He nods toward his younger companion.

"I have a cabin about 15 miles downstream from here on the west bank. You must come on over and stay the night." Without waiting for an answer, he opens the throttle and the boat leaps forward up the river.

It is late in the day when we reach the Krazy Kabin, but soon we are sitting at a long wooden table with Krazy George and Steve, who prove to be generous hosts. In no time our wet gear is drying above the wood stove, we've been shown comfortable beds for the night, and we are being plied with quantities of wine and food. A couple of hunting rifles lean against a wall and a stuffed moose head stares haughtily down.

"I hope none of you people are tree-huggers," says our host. "Any moose that comes into that clearing out front is dead – it's stone dead."

We tell Krazy George of our plans to paddle to Fort Fitzgerald. He stares into the wine glass cupped in his hands, then slowly, theatrically, shakes his head. "You people have no idea what you're getting into," he says. "If a wind gets up when you're half-way across Lake Athabasca, you're going to drown. What's more, the native people north of Fort Chipewyan hate whites. The children will throw stones at you and the adults will kill you and dump your bodies in the bush!"

Well! His comments about the dangers of crossing the lake aren't so crazy, but as for his other remark, is that the wine talking or is he just having fun at our expense? We smile but say nothing.

A couple more days' paddling and we reach the Richardson River Dunes and, not far beyond, the Embarrass Store, operated by Cathy and Larry McGinnis. We stay overnight in an old cabin, and in the morning, Cathy, one of those strong, practical women who seem able to cope with anything life throws at them, gives us clear instructions on how to find our way through the delta to Lake Athabasca.

From here the Embarrass River, a distributary of the Athabasca, branches north. It is the voyageurs' historic route to Lake Athabasca, but today is seldom used because of logjams. Instead, Cathy recommends we stick to the Athabasca's eastbound main channel, then cut back north along the Fletcher

ABOVE: *Sandra Foss paddles by the Richardson River Dunes at the southeast corner of Wood Buffalo National Park, where they form the east bank of the Athabasca River. They are part of the largest dune-field in Canada.*

FACING PAGE: *Some 18 species of neotropical wood warbler visit Alberta's boreal forest in summer including, clockwise from top left, palm warbler, Cape May warbler, yellow warbler, and magnolia warbler.*

ABOVE: *Once across Lake Athabasca, tension slips away as we reach the calmer waters of Fort Chipewyan harbour.*

FACING PAGE: *Bison in the mist. Wood Buffalo National Park was established to protect the remnant wood bison herd that inhabited the Peace-Athabasca Delta. Plains bison were later introduced, and the bison there today are hybrids. This was North America's only bison herd still preyed on by wolves, but today small, free-roaming boreal herds are being restored elsewhere, hence other wolf packs are once again learning to hunt bison.[5]*

Channel to rejoin the Embarrass further downstream. She calls her nearest neighbour, Cecil Crypstra, who owns a cabin some 40 kilometres downstream, to let him know we are coming. Cecil, too, is a kind and thoughtful host, providing us with hot showers and a dry place to sleep in his huge workshop.

The following night we reach a derelict hut on top of a steep, muddy bank. This, we've been told, is the last dry land to camp on before reaching the lake. We cook supper, using the broken door as a table top, but choose to pitch our tents outside rather than sleep in the musty hut. Next morning we're up before dawn and heading for the lake, which we expect to reach by eight o'clock. But it's past ten before the channel we've been following through tall willows widens out and Lake Athabasca lies before us.

"Look!" Marian points. "The radio tower!" Through a light mist, I can just make out the first few weighted-down pine saplings that Jumbo Fraser placed at intervals in the lake to guide small craft around the reed-beds and shifting sand; and beyond, the thin, silvery tower rising above Fort Chipewyan some 12 kilometres away. We're too late, really, to make the direct crossing with any guarantee of safety, yet the water looks calm. What to do?

I REMEMBER THE WARNING of a Newfoundland fisherman we met in a restaurant in Fort McMurray. He said he'd never been as frightened as when the wind suddenly came up while he was out fishing on Lake Athabasca. He was forced to cut his nets loose and make a dash for land through eight-foot waves, expecting any minute that the rivets would pop on his aluminium motor boat. But the pine saplings beckon and we decide to risk the direct crossing.

As usual, the pace of our party is determined by the single canoe, and this is no place for Marian and me to forge ahead. We follow the line of pine saplings until they peter out, and then, with Jumbo's words ringing in our ears, we line up on the radio tower and paddle like hell. Half-way across the lake, the wind stirs and a gentle swell begins. This is what we've been

A young black bear, still wet from a rain shower, fattens for winter on tasty chokecherries.

dreading. With some six kilometres of open water ahead of us, six behind, and no other boats in sight, this would be a terrible place to capsize a heavily laden, open canoe. Luckily, the wind doesn't increase much before we reach the first of several islands that guard Fort Chipewyan harbour. Once beyond these, the swell dissipates somewhat, and soon we can see the lodge on the hill, then some houses, the museum, and finally, at its moorings, the barge – the "Athabasca Raider," which passed us five days earlier.

We have crossed the lake in an hour and forty minutes and arrived not a moment too soon. As we haul out on a sandy beach, we feel the wind blowing more strongly against our cheeks and see whitecaps forming on the lake. Marian turns to me: "The gods smiled on us this morning."

FORT CHIPEWYAN overlooks the Peace-Athabasca Delta. It was founded in 1788 as a fur-trading centre and is the oldest continuously occupied settlement in Alberta. In summer you can get there only by plane or boat, but in winter an ice-road normally connects it to Fort McMurray. Two years earlier, we drove this road to be at the town's winter festival and watch the dogsled races with teams from as far away as Yellowknife and Canmore.

The delta is one of the largest inland freshwater deltas in the world. It lies mostly within Wood Buffalo National Park and is a Ramsar site, internationally recognized as an important wetland for waterfowl. All four North American flyways converge here: up to 400,000 birds use the delta each spring as a staging or nesting area, and a million in the fall.[6]

As the lake filled behind the new W.A.C. Bennett Dam, some 1,000 kilometres upstream on the Peace River in British Columbia, in 1967, it changed the downstream flow regime significantly. Today, thanks to the dam and climate warming combined, the summer flow is down 60 percent compared to 100 years ago and the natural two- to three-year cycle of spring break-up ice jams below the delta that used to flood its perched lake basins has ended. Only three floods have occurred in the last 40 years – the latest in 1997. Indeed, the delta's wildlife habitat has so dried out that half its waterfowl are now gone and 95 percent of its muskrats, together with the traditional hunting and trapping livelihoods of several hundred native people. Wood Buffalo National Park, which was established to save the delta's wood bison, has lost hundreds of square kilometres of high-protein sedge meadows, the bison's prime winter food. Those meadows have been replaced by silverweed and thistles, along with willow and poplar.[7]

LA RIVIÈRE DES ROCHERS is aptly named. Gone are the sandbars and willow islands of the Athabasca. Pink, crystalline, Precambrian rock of the Canadian Shield now lines the shores, topped with coniferous forest.

Rested and resupplied, we say goodbye to Dan Creurier, our kind host for the past two days, and paddle round a headland where we pick up the Rivière des Rochers. At a T-junction among the willows, a signpost sticking out of the water reading "Fort McMurray 270 kilometres" throws us off route until we figure out that it is a traffic sign intended for vehicles driving the winter road, not a boating sign!

After 75 kilometres we reach the confluence where the Rivière des Rochers joins the Peace River and they become the Slave. The Slave is a huge, intimidating river, over a kilometre wide and 22 metres deep in places, with strong eddies and currents. It carries over 80 percent of Alberta's total river flow and, in June at 6,000 cubic metres per second, about 11.5 times the flow of the North Saskatchewan River at Edmonton.[8]

Provided the river is calm, paddling with the current pushing you along at three to four knots is easy. But now a strong northern headwind gets up and in no time the river is alive with white caps from shore to shore. We fight the waves for a while, then start looking for a place to land. A cabin appears high on a rocky promontory with two aluminium motorboats moored in a bay below. We battle our way ashore and haul the canoes up on the mud. This is as far as we go today.

Two middle-aged native men appear on the deck of the cabin, dressed in well-worn jackets, jeans, thick socks, and beautiful moccasins with fur

Although red squirrels mainly eat pine cone seeds, their varied diet includes insects, birds' eggs, nestlings, berries, and mushrooms. This industrious squirrel in Elk Island National Park, a boreal forest enclave, had a hoard of some 30 mushrooms drying on branches, to be cached later for winter.

trim around the ankles. Their grey hair and weather-beaten faces tell of a lifetime outdoors. They agree to our camping among the trees near the cabin and watch as we haul our gear up the bank. The older man comes over. "We're going moose-hunting for a couple of days. Would you like to stay in the cabin?" We decline gratefully, but what extraordinary kindness. We have been with these men for only half an hour and already they're prepared to entrust us, three total strangers, with their cabin. If only Krazy George were here.

Overnight the wind dies down, the sky clears, and the river becomes a sheet of glass. The lion has become a lamb. We leave soon after dawn. At noon, halfway around a 16-kilometre meander, we stop for a snack. It is a heavenly spot, the Silent North of poets and storytellers: no motors or generators, no police sirens wailing, no helicopter rotors hammering, no stereos blaring, no "beep-beep" of construction vehicles backing up; just the tranquility of water rushing over rocks, wind sighing in the trees, and a woodpecker seeking a meal. There's an old Arab saying, "God created the desert so that he could walk in it alone, away from man." It applies equally well to the boreal forest.

BEYOND THE MEANDER LIE THE DEMICHARGE RAPIDS. The advice given us is to keep to the right shore and avoid the worst by taking a side channel behind an island before returning to the main channel. At first the side channel is calm, but rounding a rocky promontory, the current accelerates. Marian in the bow turns and shouts: "Hard left! Huge whirlpool ahead!"

We immediately try to turn, but the river's force is irresistible. Before we know it, we're sucked into a great swirling funnel of water. Paddling furiously, we avoid the hole at the centre of the vortex but beyond that have little control. Powerful forces grab our heavily laden canoe as if it were a leaf. We are spun around, then spat out backwards beyond the promontory. Here, in an eddy, we pull ashore and rest our frayed nerves.

As ghostly sunlight seeps through the morning mist, something is unfolding in the glade. A thousand tiny, silken parachutes hang inverted from shrubs or branches, each laced with winking dewdrop strobes.

Spiderlings are about to launch themselves on the whisper of a breeze, to seek their destiny.

MARIAN'S DIARY, 9 SEPTEMBER 2001

FACING PAGE: *The Salt River, Wood Buffalo National Park.*

FOLLOWING PAGES: *The beauty and variety of the boreal landscape takes our breath away as we look down from a rented bush plane. Below are the visceral meanderings of the Salt River, bordered by a halophytic (salt-loving) plant, the red samphire.*

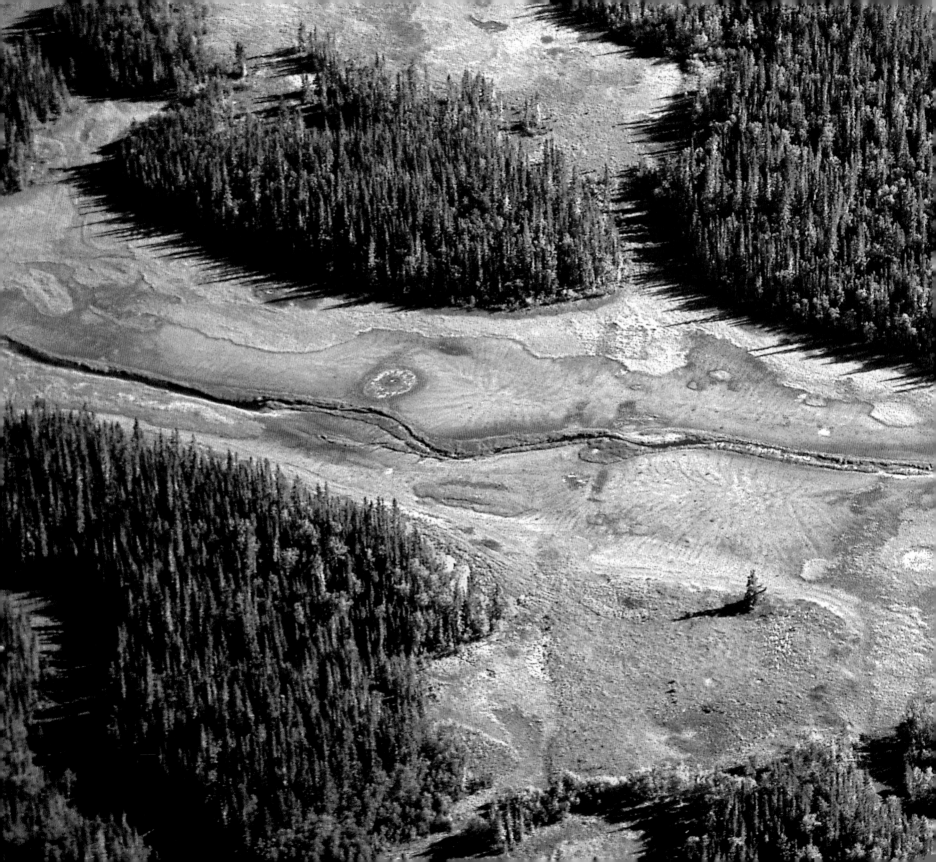

ABOVE: *Strange and beautiful plants grow in the boreal forest. Insects eat plants, but some plants in nutrient-poor terrain eat insects. One is the pitcher plant, which employs a passive pitfall trap: nectar entices insects to the lip and into the pitcher – a modified leaf. Waxy secretions and downward-pointing hairs prevent them from retreating. Eventually they fall, exhausted, and drown in digestive enzymes at the bottom. Pitchers inhabit the lower Athabasca drainage.*

FACING PAGE: *The roundleaf orchid is common in moist areas of the boreal forest.*

The next day is our fourteenth on the river, and conditions have changed dramatically since our first days on the Athabasca. Gone are our shorts, T-shirts and sun hats, replaced by long underwear and trousers, fleece jackets, woollen hats, and plastic bags over our socks to keep them dry. Whereas we never thought twice about jumping into the Athabasca to push the canoe off a sandbar, we realize that any prolonged dunk in the Slave will certainly result in hypothermia. We think about this every time the charts direct us to cross the vast river and follow some channel on the far side.

A north wind gets up and we struggle against it all the following morning. Around midday we reach Hay Landing on the western shore, then 10 kilometres further on, Stony Island. Visibility is poor, but through binoculars the route ahead, as shown on the charts, looks daunting. At the far end of the island, passage seems blocked by a line of white caps and flying spray where the strong current slams hard up against large rocks jutting east across the river. Drawing the boats together in the choppy water, we discuss our options. A motorboat, the only craft we've seen all day, ploughs upstream through the waves a kilometre away, hugging the far shore. Maybe the charts are wrong, we are thinking. Maybe we should be over there.

THIS TIME PRUDENCE WINS OUT OVER VALOUR. We pull ashore and camp among alders, hoping the weather will improve tomorrow so we can make it to Fort Fitzgerald. But the next day is worse. It rains, the north wind continues to blow, and whitecaps dance on the river. It would be madness to continue in such conditions. The second night, the temperature drops to freezing, and the morning brings no change in wind or river. What to do? Our mountaineering instincts tell us to make our food rations last a few extra days, await a break in the weather, then paddle those last few kilometres to Fort Fitzgerald. But it isn't our decision alone to make, and Sandra, in the single canoe, isn't interested in fighting this river any longer.

So, after three days of poor weather, we put our canoes back into the water and, hugging the shore, paddle back upstream to Hay Landing. From

ABOVE: *Snowshoe hare. With their thick pelts and large feet, both the lynx and its chief prey, the snowshoe hare, are precisely adapted to life in the cold and snow of the boreal forest. Records of furs and pelts traded by the Hudson Bay Company going back 200 years help researchers understand lynx-hare population cycles. Hare populations build in synchrony across the country over 8 to 11 years, peaking at up to 3,100 hares per square kilometre. Then, for reasons not fully understood, the population crashes by 80 to 90 percent.*

FACING PAGE: *Lynx. Nearly 100 years ago, naturalist Ernest Thompson Seton wrote: "Of all northern creatures, none is more dependent on rabbits than is the Canadian lynx. It lives rabbits, follows rabbits, thinks rabbits, tastes rabbits, increases with them, and on their failure dies of starvation in the unrabbited woods."*

there, Marian and I plan to route-march the 42-kilometre dirt road to Fort Fitzgerald, then hitch a lift to our camper in Fort Smith. But the long hike isn't necessary. We've been at Hay Landing only an hour when two parties of aboriginal moose hunters arrive. On hearing our story, one couple offers to delay their trip and drive us all the way to Fort Smith. Once again, the generosity of the local people to strangers is quite extraordinary. An hour and a half later we reach Fort Smith and are soon heading back in our truck to pick up Sandra and the canoes. That night over a beer, we reflect on our adventure and all we have learned from our various trips to the boreal forest.

For a couple of novices, the canoe trip itself was a real Canadian adventure. When John Semple said the area was remote, he wasn't kidding. In two weeks, all we saw – once beyond the Fort McMurray area – was one barge and a few motorboats, mostly far off. We saw no other human-powered craft. But around Fort McMurray and elsewhere in the boreal forest, outside of Wood Buffalo National Park, it's a different story. Overwhelmingly, the forest is no longer remote. It's being overrun by resource-extractive industries driven by a set of values far different from the traditional ones of the aboriginal people who live there.

FIRST NATIONS AND MÉTIS PEOPLE have a longstanding cultural attachment to the boreal forest. They adapted to its harsh conditions, and for millennia it provided them with a sustainable supply of food, clothing, shelter, and medicines. They shared a land ethic with others of their kind that said, "Consider the effects of your actions on your successors, to the seventh generation."

But considering the next generation, never mind the seventh, doesn't appear to be a priority with many people in government and industry today. They seem to see the boreal forest as a bonanza of untapped riches that, until recently, had been overlooked and were "going to waste." As if to make up for lost time, they have engaged in a massive onslaught on the forest,

converting it to pulp or bulldozing it aside to make room for tens of thousands of oil and gas wells, open-pit coal mines, and an expanding cobweb of access roads and transmission, pipe-, and seismic line rights-of-way. In its 1999 report, Canada's all-party Senate Subcommittee on the Boreal Forest was critical:

> "There is ample evidence to show that current forest use and management practices are destroying our legacy, that we are cutting too many trees over too large an area, and that our forest policies have been ill advised." [9]

THEN THERE ARE THE TAR SANDS (which spin doctors have re-labelled "oil sands"). This material comprises about 83 percent clay and sand, 5 percent water, and 11 percent bitumen (tar).

"I consider the oil sands to be the eighth wonder of the world," former premier Ralph Klein once boasted, and many Albertans share his view. The tar sands are the second largest oil reserve in the world and have become the driving force behind Alberta's economy. They are creating thousands of new jobs, and were it not for the pitifully inadequate royalties (1 percent until the development cost of a project has been recovered, then 25 percent of net revenue), the province would be far wealthier financially than it already is. But monetary wealth isn't everything.[10]

"I consider the tar sands to be an ecological holocaust," counters Dr. Richard Thomas, a boreal forest expert, a former consultant to the Alberta government, and someone with a different set of values. Most Albertans equate the tar sands project with images of monstrous machines gouging

LEFT AND FACING PAGE: *Pumping like pistons, stilt-like legs carry moose easily through deep snow or water and over deadfall in forest and woodland/grassland mosaics. Moose are great swimmers, diving up to five metres deep in lakes for aquatic plants to eat, but survive in winter on twigs of trees and shrubs. Some winters, they suffer greatly from ticks, whose blood-sucking can kill them. Global warming means more ticks.*

away at the earth in vast open-pit mines near Fort McMurray, a town "somewhere up north." What they don't realize is that those open-pit mines represent only the tip of the iceberg. The bulk of Alberta's tar sand deposits (81 percent) are buried so far underground that they will have to be mined in situ (in place) by a complicated process of steam injection. That requires the construction of myriad wells, roads, pipes, and other infrastructure over 21 percent of the province – an area as large as Florida.[11]

In a report co-authored with the Canadian Parks and Wilderness Association, the Pembina Institute came to a similar conclusion as Thomas: "It is clear that even with state-of-the-art practices, the cumulative ecological impacts of in situ development will be devastating."[12]

Pembina, and many others, are dismayed at the lack of any long-term vision for the tar sands beyond rapid development. They want a moratorium on the approval of further projects until an adequate plan is in place to manage tar sand development. That means policies and regulations that "protect the Athabasca River, address toxic tailing ponds, and ensure that industry is responsible for fully reclaiming the mines and restoring the boreal forest."[13]

For those, like Klein, who consider the tar sands a national treasure, let's do a tongue-in-cheek comparison of their public costs and benefits with those of the only survivor of the Seven Wonders of the Ancient World – Egypt's Great Pyramid of Cheops (see table, page 143).

UNTIL WE TURN A FOREST INTO LOGS, it has no value, is what many people seem to believe. But most of us disagree. For us, a biologically rich forest that has evolved over centuries is something wonderful, spiritually uplifting, and worthy of preservation in its own right.

If that isn't reason enough for protecting the boreal forest, consider *Counting Canada's Natural Capital,* a groundbreaking study by researchers at the Pembina Institute. In it, they attempted to put a dollar value on the services Canada's boreal forest provides us free of charge: flood control, pest

Wetlands control floods, filter water, and foster biodiversity. These services, worth millions and provided free by Nature, are all too often ignored or undervalued.

control, carbon sequestration, and nature-based recreational opportunities, to name a few. It came to a staggering $93 billion for 2002! That is two-and-a-half times larger than the approximate $37.8 billion value of all the timber, minerals, oil and gas, hydroelectric generation, and the like extracted from the forest that year. Ninety-three billion sounds a lot. But if that forest and peatland weren't there, the researchers calculated that the flood-control measures alone that Canada would have to take would cost some $80 billion a year.

Now the boreal forest faces a new threat. In the largest insect infestation in North American history, the pine beetle recently swept across the Rockies from British Columbia and is attacking millions of Alberta's mature pine. The government's response has been to order the felling of the affected trees. However, that doesn't stop the beetles. What it does is damage watersheds, leading to erosion and drought, and destroy valuable caribou habitat.

More beetle larvae are surviving today than in the past for two reasons: warmer winters brought on by climate change, and a decades-old but misguided policy of fire suppression, leading to an overabundance of mature pine – favourite food of the beetles.

Canada's boreal forest is a continuous green mantle and scientists fear that, when the beetles get into the jack pine, they will chew their way right across to the east coast. Furthermore, it may not be just the trees that die – so, too, may communities along the way that depend on the forest.[14]

THE ALBERTA TAR SANDS: EIGHTH WONDER OF THE WORLD?

	TAR SANDS[1]	GREAT PYRAMID OF CHEOPS
Who Owns	The people of Alberta	The people of Egypt
Who Benefits	Oil companies (mostly foreign controlled); attendant service industries; property speculators; companies and towns in the U.S. getting Alberta's raw bitumen and the thousands of Alberta up-grading jobs exported with it.[2] But tar sand royalties ($950 million in 2005–06) contributed less to provincial coffers than did gambling.	The people of Egypt. In 2005, tourism revenues were CAD$7.6 billion.[3] The Great Pyramid, and nearby Sphinx, are Egypt's most famous attractions.
Public Subsidies	At least $40 billion in federal incentives and tax breaks by 2004.[4] These, plus absurdly low provincial royalties, amount to a huge and perverse public subsidy.	Nil
Land Area Affected	In surface mining, 2–4 tonnes of sand, clay, and bitumen are dug up for each barrel of oil produced. Surface and in situ projects combined will affect 200,000 hectares (2.5 times the land area of Calgary) of complex boreal forest and wetlands. Not one hectare of that land has yet been certifiably reclaimed to economic value (such as grazing land). And as for restoration to its original state as productive, self-sustaining boreal ecosystem, that is virtually impossible.	5.2 hectares of sand
Energy Used	Each day, tar sand operations consume enough natural gas to heat 3.2 million Canadian homes for a day. Alberta has only about 8 years' worth of conventional natural gas left,[5] and using it to produce synthetic crude oil from tar sand is like turning gold into lead.	Nil
Water Used	Two to five barrels of water are withdrawn from the Athabasca River to produce one barrel of oil.	Nil
Greenhouse Gases (GHGs)	The tar sands are the single largest contributor to GHG growth in Canada. By 2010, tar sand development is expected to be Canada's largest producer of GHGs.	Nil
Major Health Hazards	Tar sand production emits nitrogen oxide and sulphur dioxide in amounts double World Health Organization guidelines. These gases can cause serious respiratory problems and are components of acid rain, a serious problem affecting rivers, lakes, and plants downwind. Also emitted are large amounts of volatile organic compounds (VOCs), which are known carcinogens and contributors to smog, asthma, and other respiratory diseases. In 2002 Alberta was in the top four states and provinces in North America for VOC emissions. At the time of writing, allegations of increased cancer rates among Fort Chipewyan residents are being investigated.	If not picked up, ice-cream wrappers dropped by tourists attract flies – a potential health hazard.
Tourism Potential	Bus trips around the tar sands to admire the world's largest toxic tailing ponds – visible from space. Whoopee!	Camel trips around Cheops to admire an engineering masterpiece
Long-term Economic Benefits	An important revenue producer for as long as tar sand crude oil is in demand and people accept the negative effects of production on the environment and on society.	An important revenue producer for perhaps another 4,000 years

1 Dan Woynillowicz, Chris Severson-Baker, and Marlo Raynolds, *Oil Sands Fever: The Environmental Implications of Canada's Oil Sands Rush* (Calgary: Pembina Institute, 2005).
2 Diana Gibson, *Taming the Tempest: An Alternate Development Strategy for Alberta* (Edmonton: Parkland Institute, May 2007).
3 Egypt State Information Service, *Year Book 2005* (Cairo: ESIS).
4 Hon. Stéphane Dion, MP (then Minister of Environment), *Speaking Notes*, House of Commons, 19 Oct 2004.
5 Alberta Energy & Utilities Board, *Alberta's Energy Reserves 2005 and Supply/Demand Outlook 2006-2015*, Report ST98-2006 (Calgary: AEUB, 2006). In 2005, new discoveries of natural gas replaced only 63 percent of the natural gas produced, down from 75 percent in 2004. The Alberta government forecasts a continued decline.

THE CANADIAN SHIELD

Bones of the Earth

Robin White

W E WERE OBLIGED TO PULL OUR CANOES out of the water at Hay Camp on the Slave River, but we couldn't, in any case, have paddled beyond Fort Fitzgerald. Between there and Fort Smith on the Alberta/Northwest Territories border, a distance of about 29 kilometres, the Slave drops 33 metres by way of four powerful rapids: the Cassette, Pelican, Mountain Portage, and Rapids of the Drowned. The last got its name over 200 years ago after five of explorer Cuthbert Grant's men drowned when their canoe capsized in the turbulent waters. These rapids have inspired awe and respect from all who have seen them, from the first aboriginal people to the most skilled whitewater paddlers of today.[1]

This stretch of the Slave is flanked by rose-pink, Precambrian granite or gneiss outcrops two billion years old that, over millennia, have been polished and scoured by glaciers and rivers. This is the Canadian Shield, the ancient geological bones of the continent – exposed here, but underlying half of Canada. The landscape is a mosaic of rock barrens; dry jack pine forest with its ground cover of bearberry, reindeer lichens, and feathermoss;

FACING PAGE: *The beautiful Precambrian granitic rock of the Canadian Shield outcrops along the banks of the Slave River.*

145

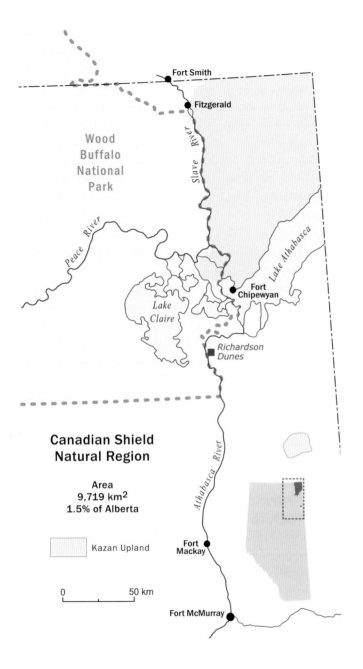

**Canadian Shield
Natural Region**

Area
9,719 km²
1.5% of Alberta

Kazan Upland

0   50 km

and soggy expanses of black spruce and tamarack with Labrador tea shrubs and peatmoss.

The Shield has a limited variety of habitats, but it is home to black bear, lynx, snowshoe hare, and red squirrels. Barren ground caribou and Arctic fox sometimes seek shelter here from the cold subarctic winter.

AMERICAN WHITE PELICANS RETURN EACH SPRING to the granite islands punctuating the rapids – the world's northernmost breeding grounds for these wonderful birds. No one knows how long they have been coming here, but explorer Alexander Mackenzie wrote about seeing them nesting at Mountain Portage Rapids in the summer of 1789. We arrive here in late September when most of the pelicans have already left for their wintering areas in the southwestern U.S., Mexico, and Caribbean. But some linger, snoozing and fishing on and around the islands.[2]

Although one of the world's largest flying birds, white pelicans are very sensitive to disturbance on their breeding grounds. If sufficiently stressed, entire nesting colonies of adult birds may leave, abandoning their eggs or chicks to starve or be preyed upon by gulls and ravens.[3] While the species is no longer listed as endangered in Alberta, the Slave River colony's breeding grounds are designated a Seasonal Wildlife Sanctuary, and it is illegal to hunt or disturb them.[4]

The number of nests on the Slave has climbed steadily, from a low of 25 in 1975 to a high of 756 in 2000; yet there's still cause for concern. Pelicans normally have two chicks, but the first-hatched usually kills its sibling, so each nest effectively produces one chick. At the Slave River colony, the number of chicks that go on to fledge varies considerably. In 2000, nearly

FACING PAGE: *American white pelicans bask on rocky islands in the Slave River near Fort Smith. The species no longer has endangered status in Alberta because the population has rebounded since the 1970s. Yet today only 6 or 7 of the 20 historic breeding sites remain in use. The main problem is human disturbance due to curiosity, recreation, industry, and commercial fishing.*

146

99 percent fledged, but in 2003 only 6.6 percent, or 46, did so out of 689 nests.[5]

The reason is unclear. Jacques van Pelt, a Fort Smith naturalist, has been studying the birds since 1974. He is a member of the Pelican Advisory Circle, which keeps careful records of the colony's breeding success. Indeed, these records are recognized as the most uninterrupted white pelican breeding records anywhere in the world.

"It seems that the chicks are being hatched," he says, "but some years – and 2003 was the worst – something happens in the first few weeks and they end up being abandoned by their parents. What it is, we don't yet know. Maybe it's small aircraft flying low over the nests as they come in to land at Fort Smith airport, or whitewater kayakers, and camera crews filming them, getting too close. Perhaps it's a combination of factors."

Matt Besko, a species-at-risk specialist with Alberta Fish and Wildlife, agrees but adds another twist: "When first hatched, the chicks are naked and the parents use their own bodies to keep them at a constant temperature – not too warm and not too cool. In 2003 we had a very hot summer. It could be that at some point the adults were seriously disturbed and flew off, and by the time they had ventured back, the chicks had fried in the hot sun."

Johnnie Desjarlais grew up on his father's trapline. We meet him one evening as we stroll along down by the Slave – a man in his late thirties, with short, dark hair and a weather-beaten face. He says he lives in a cabin on the far shore near the rapids, and although he received little formal schooling, he learned a lot about Nature by tagging along as his father attended his traplines. The two of them would camp out under the stars and his dad would sleep with his head on a beaver pelt, oblivious to prowling black bears. "It's a funny thing," Desjarlais says. "I was never afraid of bears until I went to school and the teacher told me I should be."

Desjarlais is concerned for the future of wildlife in the area. He looks across at the rapids. "If they ever go ahead with that dam, it would be the

Both male and female white pelicans grow a fibrous plate or knob on the upper bill that lasts from late winter until after the females have laid their eggs in spring. Its purpose is unknown.

end of the pelicans. And it would affect the moose and other creatures, and the people who depend on them." [6]

We know what he is referring to. Back in 1982, Alberta Environment completed a major study examining the feasibility of damming the Slave River for hydroelectric power generation. The study concluded that, while it was technically possible, the cost and environmental impacts were too great; so the project was put on hold – at least for the time being.

At sunset, we sit on the rocks overlooking Alberta's largest wild river and our conversation turns to Desjarlais' parting words.

"From what we've seen these past years, he's right to be concerned," says Marian. "If people really care about the wildlife and the environment, they can't just assume government will do the right thing. They'll have to stay vigilant and actively participate in decision-making, not only at the voting booth but between elections as well."

Larger and shaggier than crows, ravens are among the most intelligent of birds. Mutual grooming, or "allopreening," is common bird behaviour and serves to strengthen the pair bond. Ravens mate for life.

PART TWO

At the Crossroads

OLD POLITICS

Losing Our Way

SEVEN YEARS OF TRAVELLING AROUND THE PROVINCE strengthened our love of wild Alberta. But it also confirmed that Alberta urgently needs to put its environmental house in order. Certainly some progress has been made. Within Canada, Alberta is a leader in wind-power generation, sewage treatment, and electronic-waste disposal. Gas flaring and venting have been reduced substantially and the grizzly bear hunt suspended.

But Alberta has serious problems. At a time when scientists warn that climate change, freshwater shortages, overconsumption, and overpopulation are driving our planet toward ecological collapse, this province seems addicted to growth at any cost. Indeed, our per capita consumption of water and energy are among the highest in the world, as is our production of greenhouse gases.* Our ecological footprint – a measure of the demands we place upon Nature – is five times larger than the planet can sustain and 36 percent more than that of other Canadians. Being worse than other Canadians is nothing to brag about: a study of environmental performance by researchers at Simon Fraser University gave Canada a failing grade on

FACING PAGE: *Most Albertans are city-dwellers, seemingly oblivious to the rapidly changing face of wild Alberta. Is this the legacy we want to leave to our children and grandchildren?*

* Alberta accounts for 25 percent of Canada's total air pollution; also 40 percent of its GHG emissions, of which, per capita, we emit 34.2 tonnes compared to Ontarians' 6.2. Seven of Canada's top ten GHG emitters are in Alberta, where GHGs are up 40 percent since 1990. Source: Pembina Institute, *The State of Alberta's Environment* (Calgary: PI, 2006).

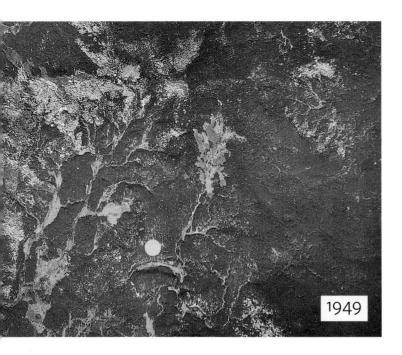

`1949`

ABOVE AND FACING PAGE: *Sacrificial zone: these two aerial photographs show an area roughly 8.5 by 6.5 kilometres in the Swan Hills (Twp. 63, Rge. 11, W5M). A yellow spot marks the same ridge in each. In 1949 the area was pristine. By 1991, oil wells (white squares), access roads (white lines), and clear-cut logging (light grey areas) had infiltrated nearly the entire area. The cumulative effect of such resource extraction is turning ever more of Alberta's pristine wilderness into a fragmented and dysfunctional industrial landscape.*

24 of 29 indicators, and an overall ranking of 28th out of 30 countries in the Organisation for Economic Co-operation and Development.[2]

Our government likes to boast that Alberta is debt free. But it isn't. For example, more than 73,000 oil and gas wells that have been certified properly abandoned have sites yet to be reclaimed – for the oldest of which the companies are not even held liable. Total reclamation liability for these could be $2.2 billion – likely far higher – and that's ignoring the pipelines and related facilities also needing reclamation, and future reclamation of the more than 200,000 wells operating today.[3]

Then there's the world's largest industrial project – the Athabasca tar sands – with its tailing ponds and wastelands. The ponds already cover more than 50 square kilometres – one relying on a dyke up to 80 metres high. No one knows how to satisfactorily reclaim these ponds and devastated lands. The National Energy Board calls the prospect "daunting." As investigative journalist Andrew Nikiforuk says, "The whole issue of reclamation is a sleeping giant in Alberta."[4]

This is deeply disturbing, for we don't see ourselves as selfish, irresponsible people. It certainly isn't what we say we want. In 2004, nearly 290,000 (10 percent of) Albertans, rural and urban, ranked environmental protection their third priority after health and education. By 2006, the environment had become Canadians' top issue.[5]

Many changes are needed if Alberta is to become a responsible steward of the land and stop passing on a colossal environmental debt to our children. New governments in Ottawa and Edmonton promise greener policies, but can they be trusted to deliver? Time will tell. Regardless, here are nine major changes that we feel would make a substantial difference.

THE DEMOCRATIC DEFICIT MUST BE FIXED. In the 2004 Alberta provincial election, only 45 percent of citizens eligible to do so bothered to vote, and of those, fewer than 47 percent voted for the winner – the Conservative Party. That means that only 21 percent – about one in five –

actually voted Conservative. Yet the party won 75 percent of the seats in the legislature. Most voters (over 53 percent) voted for one or other opposition party. But because of the first-past-the-post electoral system, the opposition parties combined garnered only 25 percent of the seats. How can that be democratic? Disenchantment with the electoral system is a systemic reason for the steady decline in voter turnout in both federal and Alberta elections. Public apathy is another.[6]

But not voting is no solution. If we are to have responsible environmental and social law and policy, we cannot be led by incompetent, short-sighted ideologues who show no real concern for the long-term public interest. We must exercise our duty as citizens and vote for people who do. And we must demand a more democratic electoral system – one based on proportional representation.

ALBERTA MUST DEVELOP A VISION OF AN ECOLOGICALLY SUSTAINABLE FUTURE and the means to achieve it. There's growing acceptance by political leaders and the public worldwide that the fossil-fuel-based, throwaway economy of the 20th century will lead to catastrophe for life on Earth in the 21st. Europe leads in developing a greener economy, with some 27 nations agreeing to cut its carbon emissions to 20 percent below 1990 levels by 2020. They've also agreed that, by then, 20 percent of Europe's energy will be derived from renewable resources such as wind and solar power.[7]

Alas, Alberta has no coherent vision of a sustainable future. Respected ecologist Dr. J. Brad Stelfox puts it this way: "We can think of Alberta today as a house under construction. Everywhere you go, you can find men and women beavering away constructing some part of it. And they can tell you what their bit will look like when it's completed: a new road, a coalbed methane plant, a residential subdivision. But not one of them can tell you what the finished house will look like. Why? Because no one has the blueprints." Without a vision and effective regional planning, we allow any industrial use anywhere, and call that "progress."[8]

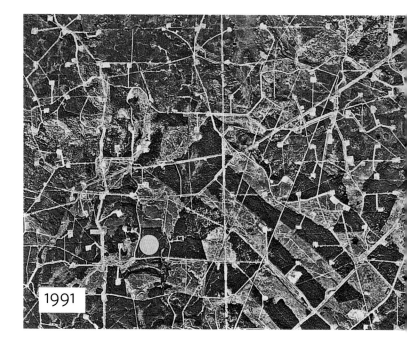

1991

Wind turbines in southern Alberta. It's high time Alberta recognized that the future lies with renewable energy and energy conservation, not fossil fuels.

ALBERTA MUST STOP SUBSIDIZING POLLUTERS. A major tool for achieving a greener economy is tax shifting. Increasingly adopted in other countries, tax shifting means reducing taxes on desired behaviour such as employment and improved energy efficiency, and raising taxes on undesirable behaviour such as releasing greenhouse gases, discharging toxic waste, generating garbage, and owning gas-guzzling vehicles.

Perversely, Alberta does the opposite. By charging among the lowest royalty rates in the world, on top of federal tax breaks of $1.4 billion per year, Alberta has been subsidizing already obscenely profitable, mostly foreign-controlled energy companies. As a consequence, Alberta has a Heritage Fund languishing at about $14 billion after 30 years of savings from oil and gas revenues, while Norway, with roughly comparable oil and gas production, has accumulated over $300 billion in its piggy bank after merely 16. At the same time, Alberta provides relatively little financial encouragement for businesses involved in renewable energy and conservation, where the future clearly lies.[9]

A BETTER METHOD OF MEASURING PROGRESS MUST BE DEVELOPED. Ever more growth seems to be the Alberta mantra, but is that what's needed to achieve a high quality of life? To find out, the Pembina Institute undertook a Genuine Progress Indicator study for Alberta. Instead of just measuring one factor – the change in the gross domestic product (GDP), the researchers examined 51 economic, social, and environmental factors over a 42-year period (1961 to 2003), including energy use, forest fragmentation, ecological footprint, gambling, and divorce rates. Their conclusion was that, while Alberta's GDP soared 400 percent over that time, our quality of life actually declined almost 20 percent.[10]

This is not surprising. Studies of well-being show that, once our basic needs are met, the answer to greater happiness isn't earning more money. We soon adapt to that and move the goalposts. Far more rewarding are family, personal development, sports, hobbies (such as learning more about wild Alberta), and community activities. These take time – which workaholics don't have.

ECOLOGICAL LITERACY MUST BECOME UNIVERSAL. Most schoolchildren today have some understanding of ecological principles. But do their parents? Many captains of industry, politicians, and economists seem to regard environmental damage as an externality to increased corporate profits and a strong economy. They don't realize – or choose to ignore – that (sunlight aside) Earth is a closed system with finite clean air, soil, freshwater, waste (including carbon) absorption capacity, and so on that together underpin our existence. If we keep degrading Planet Earth, Nature's reaction may destroy our economies, along with civilization as we know it. But if we use our intelligence to live within Nature's constraints, we can have both a healthy environment and a good quality of life.

Public education campaigns were used successfully to combat smoking and encourage seatbelt use, so why not a campaign encouraging Albertans to reduce our ecological footprint?

ENVIRONMENTAL LAW MUST BE STRENGTHENED AND ENFORCED. Laws and regulations necessary to protect the environment are usually lacking, weak, inadequately enforced, or allow politicians too much discretion. This is deliberate, and in law professor David Boyd's widely acclaimed book, *Unnatural Law*, he tells us why:

> "[Short-term] economic factors [profits, competitiveness, jobs] explain why many provincial laws allow industrial activities in parks and protected areas, why air pollution is tolerated at levels that cause thousands of premature deaths annually, ... why over-cutting and clear-cutting are still prevalent in Canada's forests, why no laws have been passed to reduce greenhouse gas emissions, why the clean-up of contaminated sites is not

A nice family get-away? While Alberta's gross domestic product has increased, the quality of life for many has declined.

... and along the McLeod, the

harlequin is teaching her young

to forage for larvae among the rapids.

Unable to fly until eight weeks old,

the seven fluffballs, hatched

just days ago, are bucking the

turbulence for all they're worth.

I'm amazed by Nature's resilience

and beauty. A perfect day.

MARIAN'S DIARY, 21 JULY 2000

FACING PAGE: *Before and after: the McLeod River valley (*TOP*), gateway to the beautiful Cardinal Divide, has been transformed by the massive Cardinal River (formerly Cheviot) mine haul-road. (*BOTTOM*): Yet no environmental impact assessment was deemed necessary for the road, despite the harm it may cause migratory birds, grizzly bears, and other wildlife due to disturbance and loss of habitat.*

required by law, why pesticides banned in other countries continue to be used in Canada, why environmental assessment laws favour development over sustainability, why laws do not protect the sources of Canadians' drinking water, why the habitat of endangered species lacks legal protection, and why laws are not enforced against known polluters."[11]

While many municipalities do better, both our federal and provincial governments rely on voluntary programs and self-regulation to protect the environment. These don't work. For example, the federal government's voluntary programs to meet its binding Kyoto Protocol target of reducing annual greenhouse gas emissions to 6 percent below 1990 levels by 2012 are failing miserably. Canada's emissions are at least 27 percent above 1990 levels.[12]

As to the adequacy of penalties and fines designed to protect the environment, one has reason to be skeptical. The Alberta logging industry fells huge areas of forest (about 65,000 hectares in 2003), and unauthorized cutting and other infractions are fairly common. Yet in 2005, fines totalled only $92,000. That's peanuts. Consider that in 2004, the fines the Calgary Public Library collected for overdue books totalled $1.4 million.[13]

MEANINGFUL PUBLIC PARTICIPATION IN DECISIONS ABOUT PUBLIC LANDS MUST BE ENSHRINED IN LAW. When in 2004 the latest bout of twinning and fencing the Trans-Canada Highway was being decided, Parks Canada held no public hearings in the Edmonton-Calgary corridor, where most Albertans live. Instead it held one open house in Calgary – on the day before the August long weekend when many people were going on holiday. That isn't meaningful public participation. As for the Province, it requires municipalities to hold well-advertised public hearings prior to decisions on zoning changes. So you'd think it would use a similarly transparent process to reach its own decisions. Well, you'd be wrong. Consider the tar sands.

To hasten their development, the Government of Alberta has happily rubber-stamped billions of dollars-worth of projects involving the destruction of vast areas of boreal forest and the depletion of a major river. Yet until recently, no broad-based public input was invited. The government seems to forget that the land is owned by the public, not foreign oil companies; that citizens provincewide have an inalienable right to a say in the future of Alberta, before, not after, such important decisions are made. Over the past decade or so, participation in "public" hearings has been limited to so-called stakeholders deemed "directly affected" by a project. Typically, the general public has merely been allowed an open house (to hear what's been decided) and invited to send in written comments. All too often, decisions have been made by a small group of politicians and bureaucrats behind closed doors, away from public scrutiny.

ALBERTA MUST START REDUCING ITS TOTAL GREENHOUSE GAS EMISSIONS IMMEDIATELY. In February 2007, the Intergovernmental Panel on Climate Change (IPCC) shook the world with its loudest warning yet on the catastrophe threatening the planet. It said that, unless we change our behaviour, average global temperatures will likely increase this century by between 1.8°C and 4°C; and much higher increases nearer the poles will transform the lives of people such as the Inuit. These predictions are truly alarming, because a 2°C increase above the pre-industrial (AD 1750) level is widely considered the threshold where self-amplifying feedback loops may make global warming unstoppable – and we are already 0.6°C of the way there.

Some people take comfort in that farmers in certain regions of Alberta may benefit from warmer temperatures in the short term. But even if they do, others will experience floods and, especially in the south, increased evaporation and severe drought. Also, diminished snow pack and melting glaciers will likely cause significant water shortages in urban areas and irrigated farmland.

ABOVE: *Coal strip mine in the Central Parkland. Almost half of Alberta's greenhouse gas emissions come from coal burnt in power plants to generate electricity; only a fifth comes from tar sands.*

FACING PAGE, TOP: *Tar sand strip mines destroy Nature's complex handiwork: streams and wetlands, living matter, the soil – a centimetre of which can take well over a hundred years to form.* BOTTOM: *None of the stripped land can likely be restored to boreal forest.*

ABOVE: *Niger, Africa. The world's poor, those least responsible for global warming, will suffer the most from it. For industrial nations, this is a moral issue.*

FACING PAGE: *The Athabasca tar sands. Greenhouse gas (GHG) emissions per barrel of synthetic crude produced have fallen substantially, but booming production makes the project the single largest contributor to the growth of Canada's GHG output. How long the frenetic pace lasts may well depend on how long citizens choose to tolerate the huge environmental and social costs.*

Meanwhile, for many of the world's poorest peoples in Africa and Asia – those least responsible for the greenhouse gas (GHG) problem – it will be a catastrophe. Increasingly, prolonged heat, severe storms, floods, and droughts will destroy crops and displace people, creating hundreds of millions of environmental refugees and even becoming the catalyst for war. Coupled with habitat loss, climate change is already causing massive species extinctions.

In a landmark study for the British government, former World Bank chief economist Sir Nicholas Stern predicts that, if unchecked, climate change will lead to a global economic downturn equivalent to the Great Depression and the First and Second World Wars combined. Climate change, then, is not just another environmental issue, it has to be treated as an international emergency.[14]

For Canadians, who are among the world's largest emitters of GHGs, this is a moral issue that should be above party politics. We must act. Canadians do not want to be seen as climate change outlaws. Reducing our GHG emissions in step with places like California and Europe must become an overarching consideration for industry and all levels of government throughout Canada.

Alberta produces 40 percent of Canada's GHG emissions – almost half of that from coal-fired power plants and a fifth from tar sands. It's time to accept that this is unsustainable and challenge ourselves to develop a low-carbon economy. That means starting now to reduce GHG emissions absolutely, phase out coal-fired power stations, and use laws and fiscal incentives to vigorously promote energy conservation and renewable energy use. We have the technology; we just have to find the courage to act.[15]

CRITICAL WILDLIFE HABITAT MUST BE PROTECTED, INCLUDING WILDLIFE CORRIDORS. Some species, such as coyote, raccoon, hare, crow, starling, and American robin, seem able to adapt to the increasing pace of industrial

Tree lichen (this one an Usnea *species) is vital winter food for woodland caribou. The lichen grows very slowly, so is abundant only in old-growth forest.*

activity and loss of habitat, but 80 percent of animals can't. As mentioned, mountain caribou, grizzly bear, sage-grouse, burrowing owl, and piping plover (pages 24, 50, 58, 61, 92) are all struggling to survive in Alberta. And the situation is likely worsening. A 2007 study by the U.S. National Audubon Society shows that many common bird species have declined by 50 percent or more over the past 40 years. Causes include loss of grassland, natural forest, and wetland habitats, plus urban sprawl and industrial agriculture.

As we explained earlier (page 51), neither Alberta's *Wildlife Act* nor Canada's SARA adequately protect the habitat of endangered and threatened species. The relationship between a species and its habitat, and the threats it faces are complex, and its best chance of recovery is when its protection is based on the best available science. Alberta should follow the U.S. and Mexico, where the list of species at risk is determined by scientists, not politicians, and their critical habitat protected by law, whether on public or private land.

Increasingly, parks are islands surrounded by highly developed land-scapes and too small to protect wildlife. So it's important that corridors of natural vegetation link them together to enable wildlife to find food, shelter, and mates. Climate change only increases this need, especially among plants, because in many places their habitat is changing faster than they can adapt. As the climate warms, many plant species will try and move toward the poles or, in mountainous regions, further upslope. This is no small issue. In his best-selling book, *The Weather Makers,* Tim Flannery warns that the extinction of 18 percent of the world's species may now be inevitable, and it could be twice as much among species that can't move fast enough or have nowhere to move to.

ENVIRONMENTAL PROTECTION MUST BE PROPERLY STAFFED AND FUNDED. Government departments and agencies often fail to perform because they are starved of funds. At Parks Canada, this led to cutbacks in trail and campsite maintenance, back-country wardens, scientific research, and natural history education programs, plus a steep rise in park entry fees. When, in 2000, an independent expert panel reviewed Parks Canada's performance, it criticized its preoccupation with revenue generation at the expense of protecting ecological integrity – its priority under the *National Parks Act*. Hopefully recent hiring will turn this around.[16]

Alberta is no different. In 1996 the government cut 600 staff positions and $123 million from the Environmental Protection Department* and has never looked back. In its 2006-07 budget, out of estimated revenues of over $23 billion, the government planned to spend only $159 million on the environment, even though that is now the public's top priority.[17]

But take heart! While our government has lost its way in managing wild Alberta – the basis of our economy – a growing number of people are finding the path to a better tomorrow.

* The word, "Protection" was then deleted from the department's name. Similarly the Energy Resources Conservation Board's name change to Energy and Utilities Board dropped the word "Conservation." The Fish & Wildlife Division has been moved from the Ministry of Environment to that of Sustainable Resource Development (along with Forestry and Public Lands divisions), and much of its work is now conducted by a charitable organization, the Alberta Conservation Association.

RIGHT, TOP: *Warden Peter Clarkson tracking harlequin ducks on the Maligne River in Jasper National Park. Severe budget and staff cutbacks have crippled our federal and provincial wildlife, park, and other staff's ability to carry out their mandate of monitoring and protecting wildlife and wildlife habitat.* BOTTOM: *A misguided policy allows this hiking trail, leading to Tonquin Valley in Jasper National Park, to be wrecked by pack trains of up to 50 horses a day, each summer. Either the pack trains should be banned or the outfitters required to pay for trail upkeep.*

> *"We're not powerless.*
> *We can, in fact, move the*
> *whole world in a different direction.*
> *We just have to care enough."*

ELIZABETH MAY, LEADER OF THE GREEN PARTY OF CANADA[1]

NEW LIFESTYLES

Finding the Path

M ANY ALBERTANS AGREE SOMETHING MUST BE DONE to put the province's environmental house in order, but they personally feel powerless to change things. The best we can do, they say, is to educate our children to be better stewards than we have been.

Well, as Elizabeth May points out, this isn't true. Worse, it's a morally unacceptable cop-out. We can't wait another 20 or 30 years to drastically reduce our greenhouse gas emissions. To do so means condemning our children and grandchildren, and hundreds of millions of people around the world, to suffer through catastrophic climate change. Is that what we want?

No, our problem is an unwillingness to do what we know is right for the planet until compelled or bribed by government to do so. Writing on climate change in the *Guardian* newspaper, journalist George Monbiot put it this way: "If the biosphere is wrecked, it will not be done by those who couldn't give a damn about it, as they now belong to a diminishing minority. It will be destroyed by nice, well-meaning, cosmopolitan people who accept the case for cutting emissions, but who won't change by one iota the way they live." [2]

FACING PAGE: *Some caribou migrate to mountain meadows in summer and back down to the foothills for winter. The Yellowstone to Yukon Conservation Initiative seeks to reconnect large landscapes so that wildlife such as caribou, grizzly bear, and wolf have sufficient room to roam and live out their lives.*

167

ABOVE: *Mule deer fawn suckling.*

FACING PAGE: *Elk on Waterton wintering grounds. Their birthing areas lie to the north, outside the protection of the park.*

Fortunately, many Albertans are willing to change and to help plan a more sustainable future. Throughout this book we've said a lot about the need to protect habitat. So let's start by looking at four inspirational projects by non-governmental organizations (NGOs) that seek ecologically sensitive management of huge areas of wild Alberta.

The Yellowstone to Yukon Conservation Initiative is a science-based land-use planning project affecting a vast area stretching for 3,200 kilometres from the Yukon/Alaska border south to Yellowstone National Park. Its goal is to ensure that wildlife populations have adequate contiguous habitat in which to live their lives and mingle their genes, while ensuring sustainable local economies in the region.

The strategy is to establish large, core reserves of wild habitat (in Alberta, the major parks), link them by natural corridors, and buffer both with compatible uses such as low-impact forestry and ranching. Y2Y is ambitious, but no pie-in-the-sky dream. It is a well-organized, well-funded umbrella group involving some 200 member organizations. Founder Harvey Locke is upbeat: "We can do this. We don't have to wring our hands and say, 'Golly, it's all going!'" [3]

The Nature Conservancy of Canada is an effective protector and manager of wildlands. A recent success is its Waterton Front Project, Canada's largest ever private conservation initiative. Thanks to the generosity of the Garfield Weston Foundation and of John and Barbara Poole of Alberta, the Conservancy worked with local landowners through purchases, leasebacks, and conservation easements, to protect 100 square kilometres around Waterton. Now, it is expanding this effort north all the way to Longview, through a program called the Last Five Miles – a reference to the last grasslands remaining today, following settlers' historic expansion west across the prairies.

The Boreal Forest Initiative is as extraordinary as Y2Y. Its goal nationwide is to maintain the cultural integrity and at least half the boreal region in large, interconnected protected areas and to ensure that industrial activity

An individual can make a difference. Falconer Wendy Slaytor (ABOVE) feeds a burrowing owl hatchling, and businessman Colin Weir (FACING PAGE) releases a Swainson's hawk back to the wild over the Oldman River. They co-founded the Alberta Birds of Prey Centre in Coaldale, near Lethbridge. Their purpose: to rehabilitate injured birds, breed the endangered owls for restoration to the wild, and educate the public about raptors through the centre and visits to schools and festivals. You can "adopt" a bird to help pay for its care and recovery (see last chapter).

in the remainder meets the highest environmental standards. The project began when a diverse group of representatives from First Nations, industry, and NGOs coalesced in 2003 as the Boreal Leadership Council. If this group is successful, it will be an outstanding example of what can be achieved through collaboration when there is a common vision.[4]

The Northern Plains Conservation Network comprises 16 conservation groups from Alberta, Saskatchewan, Montana, Wyoming, South and North Dakota, and Nebraska. Although about 99 percent of the landscape is grazed or farmed, the Network has identified the ten best examples of native grassland on the northern Great Plains large enough to accommodate a herd of free-ranging bison. It isn't just wildlife that would benefit from such reintroductions. "We believe that by restoring the biodiversity of the plains we will help restore the spirit and livelihoods of those who live and work here," says biologist Rob Gardner of the Society of Grasslands Naturalists.[5]

These are all excellent projects that would welcome your support and involvement. Their weakness, of course, is that they all depend on moral suasion, not laws and regulations, to achieve their goals. And even land ownership doesn't prevent intrusion by the oil and gas industry, since government retains and sells the subsurface rights.

How can we better walk our talk? A good – and fun – place to start is for each of us to carefully examine our own lifestyle to see how we can reduce our ecological footprint: our water, energy, and material consumption, and our use of pesticides and other toxic chemicals. Everything we do bears a price tag in terms of energy and material used; we will never have zero impact on the environment, but with some soul-searching, we can reduce it considerably. Ask yourself, "Do I really need that country cottage? That big SUV? Why not a hybrid? A hybrid would reduce my fuel bill – and my GHG emissions, too. Better yet, why not bike, use public transport, or telecommute?"

We used a diesel-powered truck-camper as an affordable, secure, all-season base camp for the journeys for this book, so we're far from perfect. But for 24 years Robin commuted to work by public transit or car-pooled. The City of Calgary's light-rail-transit system gets its electricity entirely from wind turbines, saving over 26,000 tonnes of GHGs a year.[6]

We have also reduced our environmental impact in many other ways. We compost, recycle, or re-use almost everything. We choose to live in a small home with extra insulation, a high-efficiency furnace, and low-flush toilets. All our electricity comes from wind power, and every light bulb is energy-efficient fluorescent.

For a decade we looked for an R-2000 (highly energy efficient) home, with no luck. Now, however, a new neighbourhood is being built in the Town of Okotoks that will be totally R-2000. It is the Drake Landing Solar Community, North America's first large-scale solar-heating project using seasonal storage underground to capture the sun's rays in summer to heat homes in winter. Each home will be 30 percent more energy efficient and emit 5 tonnes less GHG per year than conventional housing.[7]

We buy locally grown food from the Calgary Farmers' Market, and good-quality products that last from companies that demonstrate an environmental conscience. For example, we patronize Patagonia not just for its high-quality outdoor clothing but for its industry-leading efforts to reduce the negative effects of its operations on the environment.[8]

Mountain Equipment Co-op shares Patagonia's values and sells its products. MEC aims to become a role model of corporate responsibility in

ABOVE: *Stewardship programs: Angéle Field owns Fieldstone Bed and Breakfast by Flyingshot Lake, near Grande Prairie. She tells guests about the trumpeter swans that return each spring to nest and raise their cygnets on her secluded shoreline. Field has become a Swan Steward to preserve that habitat in its natural state, so the swans will thrive. Alberta Fish and Wildlife's Mark Heckbert adjusts the sign.*

Some 200 other Alberta landowners have signed up to protect the endangered burrowing owl. The program has now been expanded to cover loggerhead shrikes and other species, making these landowners Grassland Stewards.

Wanted! More good stewards! FACING PAGE: *Cattle drives may soon be a thing of the past. Ranchers face competition for land from farming and estate-lot development, and for market share from feedlots, which now control over half of Alberta's six million cattle. Also, many ranch children are abandoning the lifestyle. This is unfortunate because most ranchers have been excellent stewards of the land, many placing conservation easements on it to ensure long-term protection. Growing numbers are forming groups to ward off energy industry degradation of our grassland heritage.[9]*

Along the South Saskatchewan.

Canada. It has a comprehensive program with defined target dates for reducing the waste, energy, packaging, shopping bags, and paper fibre (mostly catalogues) it uses. Its Alberta stores get all their electricity from wind turbines.

A small-business example is Aurum Lodge, a posh bed-and-breakfast on Abraham Lake, west of Nordegg. Owners Alan and Madeleine Ernst do all they can to minimize the impact of their business on the environment. For this they received a five-star rating from the Audubon International Green Leaf Eco-Rating program, which is given only to "world leaders in environmental performance." The Ernsts donate 2.5 percent of their gross profits to environmental causes.[10]

We also support many not-for-profit environmental advocacy groups (see page 180) that educate the public and pressure government to keep its promises and comply with, and strengthen, its environmental laws. Foremost among these is the Alberta-based Pembina Institute, an independent environmental policy, research, and education group, whose outstanding work we have drawn upon in several chapters of this book. The Sierra Club of Canada, Canadian Parks and Wilderness Association, and Alberta Wilderness Association are some of the other groups whose efforts to protect Alberta's environment we wholeheartedly support.

All such groups need volunteers to do everything from envelope stuffing to fundraising, legal work, research, public education, and advocacy. Sure, one person's actions are a drop in the bucket, but together we can create a tidal wave of change.

FINALLY, IT'S IMPORTANT TO GET OUT AND ENJOY NATURE as often as possible – to become emotionally re-attached to it. Our society has become so urban, sedentary, and addicted to work, amusement, and selfish material consumption that most people today have little personal experience of wild places. But only with personal experience comes the passion for Nature needed to fight for it.

That passion doesn't develop from reading books or from hanging a Nature calendar on the office wall. It requires spending time sitting by a river or on a prairie bluff or mountainside, soaking in the landscape – watching the animals, the plants, the changing sky. Do this often enough and, like us, you may well reach a turning point. So when industry pollutes our air, depletes and pollutes our rivers, dismantles our old-growth forests, fills in prairie potholes, destroys critical wildlife habitat, and profits from the sale of our non-renewable natural resources at fire-sale prices, you will get angry. Angry enough to take action.

An emotional, indeed spiritual, attachment to Nature is nothing new either to our own ancestors or to Alberta's first peoples. Marian wrote in her field notebook:

> *11th October. Up early to catch the dawn. A rill trickles from the forest edge, below wild currant ablaze with autumn colours. It entices me into the forest, then leaves me alone among the peaceful gloom of spruce. I follow an animal trail awhile.*
>
> *It leads to an inner sanctuary. A solitary beam of sunlight slants down upon the trunk of a mature aspen tree at the glade's edge. There, tied with a neat knot around the white bark, are a few beautiful, long satin ribbons. A zephyr wafts and turns them gently, making a play of reflected light like the spoken words of a prayer.*
>
> *It is an intimate experience, feeling the palpable spirituality of the place, of the person who tied the ribbons, who surely prayed here. That person is someone whose people continue to honour and dignify their bond, their reciprocal ties, with the land and waters, the birds and animals, the flood and fire and seasons that nurture us all.*
>
> *Time is rapidly running out. I pray my kind will learn to rekindle that bond before it is too late.*

Prayer ribbons in the forest, placed there by someone with an abiding, spiritual attachment to the land.

175

RESOURCES

Getting Started, Striding Out

EXPLORING ALBERTA'S NATURAL HISTORY can be overwhelming if you are new to the province or have paid little attention to Nature before. The following resources can help you get started and we anticipate that, like us, you'll have a lot of fun in the process!

Backyard birding is a great way to begin, and urban, provincial, and national parks are good places to see birds, wildflowers, and other wildlife (page 178). So are nature festivals (pages 178–79). Clubs full of knowledgeable people (pages 179–80), and books (page 181) can help you on your way. Now in your stride, see page 182 for books on issues and creating positive change. For updates, see www.naturewatchworld.com. Action groups for all tastes eagerly await your involvement (pages 180–81). You'll be in good company.

ROLLING UP OUR SLEEVES and working on solutions is a job for each and every one of us, brimming with exciting new economic and personal opportunities. We have the tools. Let's get on with the job. The race is on and other countries and jurisdictions are leaving us in the dust. Can we catch up and even take the lead? Albertans, are you up to the challenge?

FACING PAGE: *Swan-watching*: *Gerard Beyersbergen (centre) of the Canadian Wildlife Service leads a group to see the trumpeter swans during Grande Prairie's Annual Swan Festival in late April. Other nature festivals are held around Alberta and nearby in British Columbia.*

Your own backyard is a good place to start. If you plant suitable trees, shrubs, and flowers, wild birds and butterflies will come. You'll see their lives unfold and change with the seasons. Bonding with Nature is life-reaffirming: when migrant birds leave us in the fall, you'll feel sad; and when those friends return in spring – why, you will be filled with joy.

National Parks
Banff, Jasper, Waterton Lakes, Elk Island, Wood Buffalo
www.parkscanada.ca

Provincial Parks
More than 500 provincial parks and "protected" areas
www1.travelalberta.com/content/parks/otherparks.cfm

City Nature Centres and Natural Areas
Ask your local naturalist group or city parks department. Here are some:
CALGARY – Fish Creek Provincial Park and Environmental Learning Centre
CALGARY – Weaselhead Glenmore Park; www.weaselhead.org (a fantastic site)
EDMONTON – John Janzen Nature Centre
GRANDE PRAIRIE – Muskosepee Park and Museum
LETHBRIDGE – Helen Schuler Coulee Centre
LLOYDMINSTER – Bud Miller All Season Park and nature trails
MEDICINE HAT – Police Point Park and Nature Centre
RED DEER – Kerry Wood Nature Centre at the Gaetz Lakes Sanctuary
TOFIELD – Beaverhill Natural Area and Nature Centre

National Migratory Bird Sanctuaries
Three are easily accessible (the fourth is in a remote, unroaded area near Lake Athabasca):
CALGARY – Inglewood Bird Sanctuary

GRANDE PRAIRIE – Saskatoon Lake NMBS at Saskatoon Island Provincial Park (20 kilometres west)
RED DEER – Gaetz Lakes Sanctuary (listed federally as the Red Deer NMBS)

Wildlife Rehabilitation Centres
Here's Canada's largest birds-of-prey facility (see www.calgarywildlife.org/links/rehab.html for others):
Alberta Birds of Prey Centre
Coaldale, AB T1M 1M9
tel 403 345-4262
email: info@burrowingowl.com
www.albertabirds.com

BELOW: *Backyard birding: In winter, Bohemian waxwings are a familiar sight in urban areas, where they descend swirling, like schools of fish, to feast on the berries of mountain ash trees. We took this picture of a waxwing in our neighbour Marilyn's tree from our bedroom window.*

Natural history festivals are great fun! Usually annual, they include guided walks or bus tours as well as talks and slide shows, displays, children's events, crafts, and of course, wildlife. Why not start one in your community? They involve work but are well worth it. And local shops, restaurants, hotels, and schools will be delighted.

Late April
Swan Festival
Saskatoon Island Provincial Park near Grande Prairie
(a weekend)
tel 780 766-2636
www.swanfestival.fanweb.ca

Early May
Wings over the Rockies Birding Festival
Invermere, British Columbia
(all week)
tel 888 933-3311 (toll free)
email wings@AdventureValley.com
www.wingsovertherockies.org

Late May
Crowsnest Wing Fest
Blairmore, Crowsnest Pass
(a weekend)
tel 403 564-5155 (Merilyn)
email merilyn@crowsnestconservation.ca
www.crowsnestconservation.ca

Early June
Songbird Festival
Lesser Slave Lake Bird Observatory
Town of Slave Lake
(a weekend)
tel 866 718-BIRD (toll free)
tel 780 849-8240
email info@borealbirdcentre.ca
www.lslbo.org/songbirdfestival.asp

NATURE AND CANOE CLUBS

Mid-June

Waterton Wildflower Festival
Waterton Lakes National Park
(10 days including Summer Solstice)
tel 800 215-2395 (toll free)
tel 403 859-2663
email tgbear@telusplanet.net
www.watertonwildflowers.com

Mid-October

Festival of Eagles
Town of Canmore
(a weekend)
tel 403 678-1878 (Chris Bartolomie)
email specialevents@canmore.ca
www.canmore.ca/living/special-events/
festival-of-eagles.html

BELOW: *Nature festivals are fun for all the family. Children are proud to display the trumpeter mobiles they make at the Grande Prairie Swan Festival.*

RIGHT: *Robin paddling the Athabasca River.*

Another neat idea is to join a nature club, learn cool facts at their gatherings, and go on hikes with members, many of whom are a mine of information about the natural world. Joining a canoe club is a great way to get a feel for our wonderful, life-giving rivers. Warning: all this is not just enjoyable, it's downright addictive.

ALBERTA

Federation of Alberta Naturalists (FAN)
(umbrella group for most Alberta nature clubs)
tel 780 427-8124
www.fanweb.ca

Alberta Recreational Canoe Association
PO Box 72026, Ottewell PO
Edmonton, AB T6B 3A7
tel 877 388-2722 (toll free)
www.abcanoekayak.org

BANFF–CANMORE

Bow Valley Naturalists
tel 403 762-4160   email mcivor@telusplanet.net

CALGARY

Nature Calgary (Calgary Field Naturalists)
tel 403 239-6444 (President)   www.cfns.fanweb.ca

Weaselhead Society
tel 403 252-6141   www.weaselhead.org

COLD LAKE–BONNYVILLE

Beaver River Naturalist Society
tel 780 639-3386 (Jeremy Neufeld)
or 780 639-3787 (Del Huget)
email BeaverRiverNaturalists@telus.net

EDMONTON

Alberta Native Plant Council
tel 780 987-3054 www.anpc.ab.ca

Edmonton Nature Club
tel 780 435-7862 (Dolores)   www.enc.fanweb.ca

EXSHAW–KANANASKIS

Bow-Kan Birders
Box 153, Exshaw, AB T0L 2C0
tel 403 673-2422 (Cliff Hansen)

continued on next page

FORT MCMURRAY

Fort McMurray Field Naturalists Society

152 Cote Bay, Fort McMurray, AB T9H 4R9
tel 780 791-2376 (Grant Henry)

FORT SASKATCHEWAN

Fort Saskatchewan Naturalist Society

tel 780 992-7963 (Alice Easton)
email stamp.allie@shaw.ca

GRANDE PRAIRIE

Peace Parkland Naturalists

tel 780 539-6102 (Margot Hervieux)
email hervieux@telusplanet.net

LAC LA BICHE

Lac La Biche Birding Society

Box 1270, Lac La Biche, AB T0A 2C0
tel 780 623-2447

LETHBRIDGE

Lethbridge Naturalists Society

tel 403 328-0036 (Diana Williams)
email info@LethbridgeNaturalistsSociety.com

MEDICINE HAT

Grasslands Naturalists

tel 403 527-2052 (Rob)
email grassnat@memlane.com

RED DEER

Red Deer River Naturalists

tel 403 347-8200 www.rdrn.fanweb.ca

STETTLER

Buffalo Lake Naturalists Club

Box 1802, Stettler, AB T0C 2L0
tel 403 742-4800 (Wilma Zurfluh)

VERMILION

Vermilion River Naturalist Club

tel 780 853-4914 (Stu Heard)
or 780 847-2677 (Iris Davies)
www.vermilioninfo.com/vrnc/

Environmental groups, land trusts, and others are there to educate us and provide a vehicle for participatory action. They champion Alberta's wildlife and environment. CPAWS and Pembina offer school programs and material. Many host talks and other events, and publish books and reports. Some engage very little in advocacy, some a lot.

Until the public elects a responsible government that provides ecologically sound land-use planning, these groups are like the little Dutch boys with fingers in the dyke – except they're already up to their necks in water. They'd certainly welcome your help and support.

AN UMBRELLA GROUP

Alberta Environmental Network

tel 780 439-1916 www.aenweb.ca

THE POLITICS AND LAW SCENE

Conservation Voters of Alberta

Non-partisan, analyzes parties' and candidates' policies.
www.conservationvoters.ab.ca

Ecojustice Canada

(former Sierra Legal Defence Fund)
Vancouver, BC
tel 604 685-5618 www.sierralegal.org

Environmental Law Centre

Edmonton
tel 780 424-5099 www.elc.ab.ca

Green Party of Alberta (in each riding)

PO BOX 61251, RPO Brentwood
Calgary, AB T2L 2K6
www.albertagreens.ca

LAND AND WATER MANAGEMENT

Alberta Stewardship Network

Publishes *Directory of Watershed Stewardship in Alberta* (free hard copy, online, CD)
tel 877 727-5276 (toll free)
www.ab.stewardshipcanada.ca

Cows and Fish (Alberta Riverine Habitat Management Program)

Calgary, Edmonton, Lethbridge, Red Deer
tel 403 381-5538 www.cowsandfish.org

Ducks Unlimited

Brooks, Calgary, Camrose, Edmonton, Grande Prairie, Hanna, Lethbridge, Medicine Hat, Red Deer, St. Paul, Wainwright
tel 780 489-2002 www.ducks.ca

Trout Unlimited

Banff, Calgary, Edmonton, Edson/Hinton, Highwood, Lethbridge, Medicine Hat, Red Deer
tel 403 346-9529 www.tucanada.org

LAND TRUSTS

Land Stewardship Centre of Canada*

Edmonton
tel 780 483-1885 www.landstewardship.org

Nature Conservancy of Canada (Alberta)

Calgary
tel 403 262-1253 www.natureconservancy.ca

Southern Alberta Land Trust Society

High River
tel 877 999-7258 (toll free) or 403 646-2600
www.salts-landtrust.org

Western Sky Land Trust

Calgary
tel 403 974-0756
www.westernskylandtrust.ca

* A great resource centre concerning private land conservancy. Here's one of their books: Curthoys, L.P. 1998. *For the Love of Alberta: Ways to Save Your Natural Heritage.* Edmonton: Federation of Alberta Naturalists.

Awareness Raising, Education, Advocacy

Alberta Wilderness Association
Calgary
tel 403 283-2025 www.albertawilderness.ca

Castle Crown Wilderness Coalition
Pincher Creek
tel 403 627-5059 www.ccwc.ab.ca

Canadian Parks & Wilderness Society
Edmonton
tel 780 432-096 www.cpaws-edmonton.org

BELOW: *An "environmental" issue is actually a people, health, and deeply moral issue.*

Canadian Parks & Wilderness Society
Calgary
tel 403 232-6686 www.cpawscalgary.org

Crowsnest Conservation Society
Crowsnest Pass
tel 403 562-8923 www.crowsnestconservation.ca

Defenders of Wildlife Canada (Alberta)
Canmore
tel 403 678-0016 www.defenderscanada.org

Jasper Environmental Association
Jasper
tel 780 852-4152 www.jasperenvironmental.org

Parkland Institute
Edmonton
Energy, water, democracy, related issues
tel 780 492-8558 www.ualberta.ca/~parkland

Pembina Institute for Appropriate Development
Calgary, Drayton Valley, Edmonton
tel 780 542-6272 www.pembina.org

Public Interest Alberta
Edmonton
Promotes democratic renewal
tel 780 420-0471 www.pialberta.org

Sierra Club of Canada – Chinook Group
Calgary
tel 403 233-7332 www.sierraclubchinook.org

Sierra Club of Canada – Prairie Chapter
Edmonton
tel 780 439-1160 www.sierraclub.ca/prairie

Southern Alberta Group for the Environment
Box 383, Lethbridge, AB T1J 3Y7
email cebradley@shaw.ca

Yellowstone to Yukon
Canmore
tel 403 609-2666 www.y2y.net

Natural History

In book- and birding stores and public libraries, you can find many excellent guidebooks, too numerous to list here, describing Alberta's plants and animals.

Gadd, Ben. 1995. *Handbook of the Canadian Rockies*. Jasper, AB: Corax Press. Excellent, encyclopedic coverage of this region's natural history and geology. An essential, well-written reference book.

Hardy, W.G., ed. 1967. *Alberta: A Natural History*. Edmonton, AB: M.G. Hurtig. An excellent overview (though dated), beautifully written. Out of print but available in public libraries.

Lynch, Wayne. 2001. *The Boreal Kingdom: Life in the Great Northern Forest*. Markham, ON: Fitzhenry and Whiteside. Canada's best-known photographer-nature writer shares his extensive knowledge, trademark humour, and fascination with biology in this through-the-seasons look at the boreal forest.

Savage, Candace. 2004. *Prairie: A Natural History*. Vancouver: Greystone Books/Douglas & McIntyre. Beautifully written, comprehensive.

Government Wildlife Web Pages

Alberta Fish & Wildlife provides information about wildlife species, including reports on their status (at risk, etc): srd.alberta.ca/fishwildlife/wildlifeinalberta.

Canadian Wildlife Service and Canadian Wildlife Federation. *Hinterland Who's Who*. Lots of information about wildlife, issues, etc. www.hww.ca.

ECONOMICS, POLITICS, LAW, AND PROPAGANDA

Green Economics and Activism

Chouinard, Yvon. 2005, 2006. *Let My People Go Surfing: The Education of a Reluctant Businessman*. London: Penguin Books. Patagonia owner/CEO Chouinard is an excellent role model for operating an environmentally responsible and profitable business.

Hawken, Paul. 1993. *The Ecology of Commerce: A Declaration of Sustainability*. New York: HarperCollins. A landmark book for the 21st century – "a practical blueprint for a prosperous, sustainable future."

May, Elizabeth. 2006. *How to Save the World in Your Spare Time*. Toronto: Key Porter Books. Entertainingly written, one of Canada's most experienced environmental advocates shows how to get organized and win your social or environmental battles.

Politics and Law

Boyd, David R. 2003. *Unnatural Law: Rethinking Canadian Environmental Law and Policy*. Vancouver: UBC Press. The most comprehensive analysis available on the disastrous mismanagement of Canada's environment and what we should do about it.

Democracy Watch (www.dwatch.ca) is Canada's leading citizen group advocating democratic reform, government accountability, and corporate responsibility. Its aim is to bring government and business into line with effective modern democratic principles, thereby empowering Canadian citizens.

Harrison, Trevor, ed. 2005. *The Return of the Trojan Horse: Alberta and the New World (Dis)order*. London: Black Rose Books, with Edmonton: Parkland Institute. A compilation of essays that unmask the visionless mismanagement of Alberta by the Klein Conservatives.

Kennedy, Robert F. 2004. *Crimes against Nature: How George W. Bush and His Corporate Pals Are Plundering the Country and Highjacking Our Democracy*. Toronto: HarperCollins. A horrific account of what happens to the environment when neo-conservative ideology and corporate greed dictate public policy. A good book for Canadians to ponder, especially fans of deep integration with the U.S.

Searle, Rick. 2000. *Phantom Parks: The Struggle to Save Canada's National Parks*. Toronto: Key Porter Books. A wake-up call about how Parks Canada is failing to protect our national parks.

Propaganda Exposed

Hoggan, Jim. This company president was "so appalled at the deliberate manipulation of public opinion" by fellow public relations people that he launched a website to debunk the global warming sceptics: **www.DeSmogBlog.com**.

Monbiot, 2006. *Heat* (chapter 2); details below.

ISSUES AND SOLUTIONS*
NATURE AND THE HUMAN FOOTPRINT

Our Dependence upon Nature

Daily, Gretchen, ed. 1997. *Nature's Services: Societal Dependence on Natural Ecosystems*. Washington, DC: Island Press. Explains the numerous services Nature provides us for free.

Louv, Richard. 2006. *Last Child in the Woods: Saving Our Children from Nature-Deficit Disorder*. Chapel Hill, NC: Algonquin Books/Div. of Workman Publishing. A groundbreaking work linking disturbing childhood trends to the absence of Nature in children's lives.

Climate Change and Human Footprint

Flannery, Tim. 2005. *The Weather Makers: How We Are Changing the Climate and What It Means for Life on Earth*. Toronto: HarperCollins Canada. Considered one of the best written and most convincing books to date on the climate change problem.

Gore, Al. 2006. *An Inconvenient Truth: The Planetary Emergency of Global Warming and What We Can Do about It*. New York: W.W. Norton. Al Gore's personal quest to get nations to address climate change before it is too late. It is a book, a film, and a DVD, all best sellers, each with superb graphics.

Monbiot, George. 2006. *Heat: How to Stop the Planet from Burning*. Scarborough, ON: Doubleday Canada. A brilliant analysis of global warming and how greenhouse gas emissions can be reduced by 90 percent by 2030; **www.monbiot.com**.

Wackernagel, Mathis, and William Rees. 1996. *Our Ecological Footprint: Reducing Human Impact on the Earth*. Gabriola Island, BC: New Society Publishers. A highly acclaimed tool for measuring carrying capacity, resource use, and waste, with simple graphics.

Forestry and Agriculture

May, Elizabeth. 2005. *At the Cutting Edge: The Crisis in Canada's Forests*. Toronto: Key Porter Books. An outspoken province-by-province review of what's wrong with Canada's logging industry.

Pawlick, Thomas. 2006. *The End of Food: How the Food Industry Is Destroying Our Food Supply – and What You Can Do about It*. Vancouver: Greystone Books/Douglas & McIntyre.

Schneider, Richard. 2002. *Alternative Futures: Alberta's Boreal Forest at a Crossroads*. Edmonton: The Alberta Centre for Boreal Studies. Essential reading for anyone interested in the future of Alberta's boreal forest.

* A variety of magazines, newsletters, and tabloids are published by the NGOs already mentioned. Mainstream magazines that from time to time carry articles about nature and related issues in Alberta or Canada-wide include *Alberta Views*, *Canadian Geographic*, and *Canadian Wildlife*. The on-line *EnviroZine* is a mine of helpful information.

ACKNOWLEDGEMENTS

Both Alberta and this project proved larger and more daunting than anything we had imagined. The three years we originally allocated morphed into seven. And then we wrote the book, for which we relied upon the generous advice of a host of scientists, naturalists, conservationists, and government experts. So we have many people to thank:

First, Wendy Francis and Harvey Locke (CPAWS/Y2Y), Karsten Heuer (Parks Canada), Bart Robinson (Biosphere Institute of the Bow Valley), and Cliff Wallis (Cottonwood Consultants) for their initial encouragement and for steering us onto the right track. Rob Gardner (Grasslands Naturalists), Elida Harris and François and Danuta Montandon (Calgary), and Aileen Pelzer and Gus Yaki (Nature Calgary) provided thoughtful comments on the first good draft, and Barbara and ornithologist Peter Sherrington's advice spawned major changes.

Ricardo Acuña and Diana Gibson (Parkland Institute), David and Linda Anderson (Calgary), Connie Bresnahan (Athabasca Bioregional Society, Hinton), naturalists Ben and Cia Gadd, and André Gareau (Canmore) reviewed the second draft and really moved us ahead.

We are especially indebted to Christyann Olson (AWA) for placing editorial services at our disposal. Journalist Andrew Nikiforuk read manuscript three and generously agreed to write the foreword.

Many experts provided material and went back and forth with us to ensure accuracy. On woodland caribou, thanks to Jill Seaton (Jasper Environmental Association), Glen Semenchuk (FAN), and Cliff Wallis. On plants, Lorna Allen, Joyce Gould, and colleagues (Alberta Natural Heritage Information Centre). And on river basins, Dr. David Schindler (University of Alberta).

On the mountains, Wes Bradford (Parks Canada), Drs. Tony Clevenger (consultant to Parks Canada), Mike Demuth (Geological Survey of Canada), and Tracey Henderson (Grizzly Bear Alliance); Judy Huntley, Dr. David Sheppard, and James Tweedie (Castle-Crown Wilderness Coalition); and Dave Poulton (CPAWS).

On prairie and parkland, Cliff Wallis for his encyclopaedic knowledge; Reg Arbuckle (Ducks Unlimited/Alberta Parks), Gerard Beyersbergen (Canadian Wildlife Service), and Richard Quinlan (Alberta Fish & Wildlife) on swans; Dr. Cameron Aldridge (Colorado State University), Cheryl Bradley and Reg Ernst (Lethbridge), and Nigel Douglas (AWA); Leo Dubé, Dale Eslinger, and colleagues (Alberta Fish & Wildlife); Lorne Fitch (Cows and Fish) and Rob Gardner; Drs. Dan Johnson and Stewart Rood (University of Lethbridge); Lisa Priestley (Beaverhill Bird Observatory); and Dr. Anthony Russell (University of Calgary).

On the foothills, Dianne Pachal (Sierra Club of Canada) and Helene Walsh (CPAWS). On the boreal forest, Brian Johns (Canadian Wildlife Service), Dr. Derek Johnson (Canadian Forest Service), Stuart Macmillan (Wood Buffalo National Park), and Dr. Richard Thomas (private consultant); and on the tar sands, Dan Woynillowicz (Pembina Institute). On Slave River pelicans, Mike Besko and Jacques van Pelt.

On "Losing Our Way," Darlene Howatt (Alberta Environment) and Dr. J. Brad Stelfox (Forem Technologies).

Special thanks go to our production team who magically transformed manuscript into book form: Frances Hunter for her dedication and artistry in designing the book, Robin Poitras (Calgary) for his superb maps, and Joyce Hildebrand (AWA) for her eagle-eyed editing.

Our heartfelt thanks to them all and others besides. If our book succeeds in motivating Albertans to protect our wild heritage, it will be in no small measure due to these experts. And if any errors remain, they are our responsibility alone.

In the field we generally work alone. However, we wish to thank photographer Florian Schultz for his companionship and optimism in the backcountry – "Don't worry, that grizzly isn't interested in us." We are especially grateful to LightHawk volunteer pilot Dr. Reg Goodwin who, at his own expense, flew up from Helena, Montana and took us over the Cheviot mine.

Our sincere thanks, also, to the ranchers and others who welcomed us into their homes or onto their property to study and photograph wildlife and the land.

Lastly, we thank Marian's mother, Doris Cook, for waiting so patiently for our project to bear fruit, and Robin's mother, Sunny White, for her ongoing support of our efforts. Sunny really wanted us to write a book about our world travels but she will have to settle for this instead.

NOTES

PREFACE – TURNING POINT

1 Bear, lynx, boar, wolf: Peter Mass, Extinct Animals of the British Isles, www.petermaas.nl/extinct/britishisles.htm. Beaver: www.answers.com/topic/european-beaver. Sparrows: Food Scarcity is Hitting Sparrows (U.K.: BBC News, 9 February 2006). "Between 1977 and 2000, house sparrow numbers in the U.K. declined by 65 percent." Bees: Graham Satchell, Bumblebees Could Face Extinction (U.K.: BBC News, 5 May 2001). Three of the 19 U.K. species are now extinct and 9 more are critically endangered. "The future of a whole host of crops [could be at stake]."

MOUNTAINS – ON THE ROCKS

1 D. Hervieux et al., *Alberta Woodland Caribou Recovery Plan 2004/05 – 2013/14*, ASAR Plan #4 (Edmonton: ASRD/FWD, 2005). Also Cliff Wallis, pers. comm., 9 April 2006. Swan Hills caribou: Neil W.W. Gilliat, *Watch Over the Forest* (Edmonton: Brightest Pebble Publishing, 1999) and Tom Roschkov, *Stick-Handling through the Swan Hills* (2002), www.brassmonkeyproductions.com/grizzly/Part2.html. Tar sand effect: Richard Schneider and Simon Dyer, *Death by a Thousand Cuts: Impacts of In Situ Oil Sands Development on Alberta's Boreal Forest*, Oil Sands Fever Series (Alberta: Canadian Parks and Wilderness Society and the Pembina Institute, 2006), 14-15. Herds facing extirpation: David Hervieux, pers. comm., April 2006, and E. Dzus, *Status of the Woodland Caribou ...* (Edmonton: Alberta Environment/Fish and Wildlife, and Alberta Conservation Association, 2001), WS Report No. 30. South Jasper herd: Sierra Club of Canada, *A Review of South Jasper National Park Caribou Action Plan for Caribou Recovery Phase 1, 2005* (Ottawa, ON: SCC, September 2005).

2 Athabasca Glacier (graph, c. 1996): M. Brugman, "Glacier Terminus Fluctuations, 1700-1995," *Glaciers in Canada* (Environment Canada, Cryosystems Education Section, 23 August 2002), www.msc.ec.gc.ca/crysys/education/glaciers/glaciers_edu_e.cfm; and R. Kucera, *Exploring the Columbia Icefield* (Calgary: High Country Colour, 1999), 30. North Sask. River basin: Mike N. Demuth and A. Pietroniro, *The Impact of Climate Change on the Glaciers of the Canadian Rocky Mountain Eastern Slopes ...Phase 1: Headwaters of the North Saskatchewan River Basin* (Ottawa: NRC Geological Survey of Canada, and Saskatoon, SK: Environment Canada – National Water Research Institute, 2003).

3 Rick Searle, *Phantom Parks: The Struggle to Save Canada's National Parks* (Toronto: Key Porter Books, 2000), 51, 53.

4 Road kills: Anthony Clevenger, pers. comm., 15 November 2006. Jasper rail-kills: Wes Bradford, Jasper National Park, pers. comm., 15 November 2006. Banff rail-kills: Ken Roberge, CPR, pers. comm., 16 November 2006. Also Jim Pissot, *Spilled Grain, Dead Bears, and Hollow Excuses: The New Canadian Pacific Railway Trilogy* (Canmore: Defenders of Wildlife Canada, 2006).

5 Jim Bertwistle, Parks Canada, pers. comm., 2001.

6 Parks Canada, *Trans-Canada Highway Twinning Project: Phase 3B*, a public information session (Banff, AB: PC, April 2004). Also Anthony Clevenger, *Roads and Wildlife in the Canadian Rocky Mountain Parks: Movements, Mortality and Mitigation* (October 2002), pc.gc.ca/pn-np/ab/banff/docs/routes/chap6/routes6_e.asp.

7 Structure use: Anthony Clevenger, pers. comm., November 2006. Other choices: Grizzly preferences: Michael Gibeau and Stephen Herrero, "Roads, Rails, and Grizzly Bears in the Bow River Valley, Alberta," in G.L. Evink, ed., *Proceedings of the International Conference on Ecology and Transportation, Florida* (Tallahassee, FL: Dept. of Transportation, 1998).

8 Allan Connery, "Canmore or Crowsnest?" In *Western Investor*, February 2004. Canmore has 11,500 permanent residents, plus 3,000 homes owned by non-residents. Many of the latter houses are unoccupied most of the time. Three Sisters: David Poulton, Canadian Parks and Wilderness Society, pers. comm., 15 February 2006.

9 Canadian Parks and Wilderness Society, *Action Alert: Spray Lake Sawmills Needs Public Input* (Calgary: CPAWS, 4 May 2005).

10 Bob Blaxley, *The Whaleback: A Walking Guide* (Calgary: Rocky Mountain Books, 1997).

11 Amy Steele, "Plan to Allow Off-Road Users into Whaleback Angers AWA," *FFWD Weekly*, 19 February 2004.

12 David Sheppard, interviewed by authors (Beaver Mines, AB, 18 November 1999).

13 J. Zgurski, *The Behaviour, Evolution, and Ecology of Wolves* (2005), canidae.ca/ENDANG2.htm. Also Alberta Sustainable Resource Development, Bear Problems and Management (Edmonton: ASRD, 24 February 2004), 6, www.srd.gov.ab.ca/fishwildlife/wildlifeinalberta/bearsalberta/problems.aspx.

14 Kevin Timoney, *Environmentally Significant Areas Inventory of the Rocky Mountain Natural Region of Alberta: Final Report* (Sherwood Park, AB: Treeline Ecological Research, for Edmonton: Alberta Environmental Protection, 17 January 1998).

15 Gordon Stenhouse, Mark Boyce, and John Boulanger, *Report on Alberta Grizzly Bear Assessment of Allocation*, 2003. Their update: *Amended Report on Alberta Grizzly Bear Assessment of Allocation*, commissioned for the Minister of Sustainable Resource Development (Edmonton: 2005). Dr. Tracey Henderson, email, 14 June 2007. Backgrounder on Alberta Grizzly Bear Population, May 2007, www.grizzlybearalliance.org.

16 Central Rockies: J. Brad Stelfox, Stephen Herrero, and Delinda Ryerson, "Human Land Uses and Population Growth: Implications [for Central Rockies Ecosystem] Grizzlies," in *Final Report of the Eastern Slopes Grizzly Bear Project* (Calgary: University of Calgary, 2005), chapter 13. Whaleback area: J. Brad Stelfox, *Southern Foothills Study, Phase 1 Report* (Bragg Creek, AB: Forem Technologies, 2006), summarized by Nigel Douglas, "Cumulative Effects Study Fills Gap in South[ern] Eastern Slopes Planning," *Wild Lands Advocate* (2006) 14(5): 3-14.

17 Environment Canada, *The Accord for the Protection of Species at Risk – Backgrounder*.

18 Canadian Nature, "Listing Problems and Growing Pains in Recovery Efforts," *Canadian Nature Network Report Card 2004*, 2.

19 See srd.alberta.ca/fishwildlife/escc for membership of Alberta's Endangered Species Conservation Committee.

20 Ministerial discretion: Alberta Sustainable Resource Development, *Alberta and Its Species at Risk* (Edmonton: ASRD, 2003). Also Wendy Francis, "Endangered Species Protection in Alberta: Where's the Beef?" in *Proc. Biology and Management of Species and Habitats at Risk, Kamloops, 15-19 February 1999* (Victoria, BC: Ministry of Environment, 2000).

GRASSLAND – HONED BY THE WIND

1 Candace Savage, *Prairie: A Natural History* (Vancouver: Greystone/Douglas & McIntyre, 2004).

2 Lynn Fulton, *What about Sagebrush?* (Richland, WA: Pacific Northwest National Laboratory, science-ed.pnl.gov/pals/resource/cards/sagebrush.stm, last update February 2007).

3 John Palliser's report, mentioned in www.thecanadianencyclopedia.com's "Drought in Palliser's Triangle" web pages. In his 1863 report, John Palliser maintained that the extension of the Great American Desert into British North America was a barrier to continuous western settlement.

4 Glen P. Semenchuk, ed., *The Atlas of Breeding Birds of Alberta* (Edmonton: Federation of Alberta Naturalists, 1992). A new edition will be published in 2007.

5 S. Wilson, Mary Griffiths, and Mark Anielski, *The Alberta GPI Accounts: Wetlands and Peatlands, Report #23* (Calgary: the Pembina Institute, 2001) and Anielski, Griffiths, David Pollock, Amy Taylor, Jeff Wilson, and Sara Wilson, *Alberta Sustainability Trends 2000: The Genuine Progress Indicators Report 1961 to 1999* (Calgary: the Pembina Institute, 2001). City of Calgary, Parks Department, Wetland Conservation Plan (Calgary: CC, 17 May 2004).

6 Rob Gardner, Grasslands Naturalists, Medicine Hat, pers. comm., 4 August 2006.

7 Recent habitat change: Leo Dubé, Alberta SRD/Fish and Wildlife, Lethbridge, pers. comm., 2006. Kim Morton, pers. comm., August 2006; lek #68-9 had 48 males in 1968, 36 in 1989, 1 in 2000, and none ever since.

8 C.L. Aldridge, pers. comm., 29 October 2006, and Aldridge, "Do Sage Grouse Have a Future in Canada?" *Proceedings of the 6th Prairie Conservation and Endangered Species Conference* (Winnipeg, MB, 22-25 February 2001), 1-11.

9 About 2 million hectares or one-twentieth of public land in Alberta is leased for grazing. A (2003) Alberta law forces recreational users to obtain permission from the grazing or agricultural leaseholder. But it's a good idea to do that anyway: there may be cattle at large or prohibited access due to a fire ban. You may find contact details on a fence sign, ask permission at the ranch house concerned, or phone toll free (RITE # 310-0000) and ask for Sustainable Resource Development's Land Branch.

10 Dan Johnson, pers. comm., 24 April 2007. His 1996 study analyzed 200 regurgitated owl pellets from the Canadian prairies, including the Regina and Hanna areas. Johnson is a professor of environmental science at the University of Lethbridge and a leading grasshopper expert.

11 Stewards: Canadian Wildlife Service, Edmonton: scientist Geoff Holroyd, pers. comm., 6 April 2006. Burrows: Kevin Van Tighem, "Save the Gopher," *Environment Views* (1995) 18(1): 16-19.

12 Lorna Allen, senior community ecologist, Alberta Natural Heritage Information Centre, Edmonton, AB, pers. comm., 24 July 2006.

13 Privatization at Writing-on-Stone Provincial Park: A WoS summer park interpreter, pers. comm., May 2000. Take-back of control: Greg Ottway, a WoS summer-seasonal conservation officer, pers. comm., 12 August 2006.

14 These lands remain fragile. Farms abandoned when owners couldn't pay their taxes reverted to the Alberta government. It took action to stem population loss, restore municipal good governance, and reclaim the land. In 1938, it passed the provincial *Special Areas Act*, under which the region is governed as one giant municipality, comprising three Special Areas administered by the Special Areas Board – a Crown agency. Remaining private landowners were reassigned land, logically based on water availability. Sixty percent of the region's 2 million hectares is Crown and tax recovery land, carefully managed through leasing and community pasture arrangements. Special Areas history: www.specialareas.ab.ca/prod02.htm. See also Jack Gorman, *A Land Reclaimed: A Story of the Special Areas in Alberta* (Red Deer, AB: Gorman & Gorman, 1988).

15 Dylan Biggs, interview with authors, 14 July 2004.

16 The western blue flag was first discovered in Alberta in 1964. By 1987, eight sites were known, two of which people had destroyed and three altered. So in 1990, COSEWIC listed the iris federally as threatened. The Endangered Species Conservation Committee's *First Report* (Edmonton: Alberta Sustainable Resource Development, June 2000): 20, states that between 1987 and 1998, Alberta's known natural blue flag population at the remaining six sites decreased by 27 percent per decade.

17 John Rintoul, coordinator, Alberta Natural Heritage Information Centre, Edmonton, pers. comm., 5 April 2006.

18 Icon: Candace Savage, *Prairie: A Natural History* (Vancouver: Greystone Books/Douglas & McIntyre, 2004), 140. Hunting: W.G. Hardy, ed., *Alberta: A Natural History* (Edmonton: Hurtig Publishers, 1967), 106. Population today: Dale Eslinger, pers. comm., August 1006. The two national parks were Nemiskam, east of Foremost, and Wawaskesy in the Middle Sandhills, southwest of Empress.

19 Dams and weirs: Dr. Stewart Rood, "Impacts from Damming the Oldman River," *WISE Series, Part 2*, Program #111, Item 1, Innovation Alberta, CKUA Radio interview, 20 January 2004. Cottonwoods in trouble: Rood, interview with the author, 13 April 2005.

20 David R. Boyd, *Unnatural Law, Rethinking Canadian Environmental Law and Policy* (Vancouver: UBC Press, 2003): 44 and 159; and Jack Glen, *Once Upon an Oldman: Special Interest Politics and the Oldman River Dam* (Vancouver: UBC Press, 2000). The Alberta government began building the dam despite its own Environmental Council's determining that the dam was not needed (Glen, 33), without the required public notice or consultation, without the required federal environmental impact assessment, without legitimate federal and provincial licences (Glen, 54-55), and despite provincial and federal court rulings in favour of the dam's opponents. A federal panel concluded that the half-built dam should be decommissioned. The Alberta government completed the dam anyway.

21 Rood, pers. comm., 15 November 2006. The huge 1995 flood also resulted in countless cottonwood saplings getting established in the Bow River floodplain, although a smaller flood in June 2005 scoured many of them away. Also, a severe late-spring storm in 2005 in southern Alberta and Montana caused cottonwoods to abort their catkins, so the flood that year was of little avail. Rood's PhD student Maggie Romuld is performing the Red Deer River and dam-effects study.

22 David Schindler, pers. comm., 17 October 2006. See also Schindler and W.F. Donahue, "An Impending Water Crisis in Canada's Western Prairie Provinces," *Proceedings of the National Academy of Sciences* (10 April 2006): 1-7, www.pnas.org/cgi/doi/10.1073/pnas.0601568103; and Schindler, "High and Dry," *Alberta Views* (May/June 2003): 48-51.

23 Time to decide: Schindler, "High and Dry," 51.

24 Lost cottonwood forest: Anon, "Growing Wild: The Riverine Zone" in Utah's *Project WILD* Newsletter, Fall 1996. Pers. comm., 2006, Lorne Fitch, Cows and Fish program biologist. The program, a collaboration between the beef industry, government, and Trout Unlimited, educates landowners and others about good riverine land management practices.

25 Robb Watt, Waterton Lakes National Park warden, pers. comm., 1 August 2006.

26 Nature Conservancy Canada, *Bison Reintroduction at Old Man on His Back* (December 2003), www.natureconservancy.ca. Colin Schmidt, Grasslands National Park, pers. comm., 12 October 2006.

27 Alberta Wilderness Association, "Wild Bison Recovery Endangered: Government Fails to Add Threatened Plains Bison to Species at Risk List," news release, 18 May 2005; Don Gayton, "The Grass and the Buffalo," in *The Wheatgrass Mechanism: Science and Imagination in the Western Canadian Landscape* (Saskatoon, SK: Fifth House, 1990), 99-108.

28 Convention: Boyd, *Unnatural Law*, 166. Performance: Boyd, *Sustainability within a Generation* (Vancouver: David Suzuki Foundation, 2004).

29 Boyd, *Unnatural Law*, 173.

30 Percentage: D.J. Downing and W.W. Pettapiece, *Natural Regions and Subregions of Alberta, Pub. No.*

T/852 (Edmonton: Alberta Natural Regions Committee, 2005). Lack of protection: S. Fluker and David Poulton, *A Short Guide to Protected Areas Designations in Alberta* (Calgary: Calgary Parks and Wilderness Society, September 2002). Boundaries: Boyd, *Unnatural Law*, 175.

31 David Poulton, "The Law of Parks and Protected Areas in Alberta," *LawNow* (Edmonton: University of Alberta Faculty of Law), Aug./Sept.1999.

PARKLAND – HEARTLAND HOME

1 Ron Bjorge, Alberta Fish and Wildlife, Red Deer, "Parkland: Forgotten Natural Region," presentation to the Alberta Wilderness Association, Calgary, 9 November 2004.

2 Peter Fidler, *A Look at Peter Fidler's Journal: Journal of a Journey Over Land from Buckingham House to the Rocky Mountains in 1792 and 93*, Bruce Haig, ed. (Lethbridge, AB: Historical Resource Centre, 1991).

3 Hardy, *Alberta: A Natural History*, 296, 303-306; James MacGregor, *Behold the Shining Mountains: Being an Account of the Travels of Anthony Henday, 1754-55 – The First White Man to Enter Alberta* (Edmonton: Applied Arts Products Ltd., 1954).

4 Pioneer Alberta bluebird trails: farmer Charlie Ellis's near Red Deer, 1956; Junior Naturalists founder Joy Finlayson's, Edmonton area, 1971; Harold Pinel's, Calgary area, 1973; Duncan Mackintosh's, Lethbridge, 1974; http://audubon-omaha.org/bbbox/history2.htm.

5 Interventions at Mountain View public meeting, Feb. 2001, and publicized letters to Council. Craig Smith quoted by Gerald Gauthier, "Cardston Co. Looking to Amend Land-Use Bylaw," *Lethbridge Herald*, 11 Feb. 2003. Smith noted 63 studies showing rural sprawl unable to pay its own way; see Smith's letter to the editor, "Poorly Planned Subdivision May Threaten Fine Ranchland," *Lethbridge Herald*, 11 Feb. 2003.

6 Cheryl Bradley, pers. comm., 15 March 2001, relayed quotations from a transcript of the council meeting at which the development was approved.

7 Energy and Utilities Board, *Alberta's Energy Reserves 2006 and Supply/Demand Outlook 2007-2016*, Report ST98-2007. Andrew Nikiforuk, "Life inside a Science Project," *Globe and Mail News*, 19 April 2005. Nigel Douglas, "Carpet-Bombing Alberta's Fragile Rangelands," *Wild Lands Advocate* (2005) 13(4): 17-18.

8 Andrew Nikiforuk, "The Coming Energy Crisis," *Mid-day Express* (CBC Radio, Feb. 2005) transcript. Shirley Bray, "Coal Bed Methane Comes to Rumsey," *Wild*

Lands Advocate (2004) 12(6): 1-5. Densities: Livingstone Landowners Group, Fact Sheet, 25 July 2005. Well footprint: Nikiforuk, "Life inside a Science Project."

9 EUB Bulletin 2006-24, 7 July 2006. Andrew Nikiforuk, pers. comm., 29 June 2007.

10 Alberta Wilderness Association, "Protected Area Slated for Coal Bed Methane Development," News Release, 13 October 2004. Cliff Wallis, pers. comm., 14 November 2006. Andrew Nikiforuk, pers. comm., 29 June 2007.

11 Yellowstone swans: Winston E. Banko, *The Trumpeter Swan: Its History, Habits, and Population in the United States*, North American Fauna No. 63 (Washington, DC: US Fish and Wildlife Service, 1960, reprinted (Lincoln and London: A Bison Book/University of Nebraska Press, 1980). Grande Prairie remnant flock: M.L. James, *Status of the Trumpeter Swan ... in Alberta*. WS Report No. 26. (Edmonton: Alberta Environment/Fish Wildlife and Alberta Conservation Association, 2000).

12 Beth Sheehan, retired Grande Prairie farmer, pers. comm., 10 May 2007. Fields wet in spring when the trumpeters reach their Peace Parkland breeding grounds are vital for the swans until the ice melts from the lakes they will use. But farmers' fields are being gobbled up by expanding urban areas.

13 Grassland: Margot Hervieux, *Survey of Native Grassland Butterflies in the Peace Parkland Region of Northwestern Alberta – 2001*, SAR Report No. 47 (Edmonton: ASRD/Fish and Wildlife, May 2002), vii. Wetlands: Hervieux, *Grande Prairie Trumpeter Swan Important Bird Area Conservation Plan* (Grande Prairie, AB: Canadian Nature Federation, Bird Studies Canada, and Federation of Alberta Naturalists, Spring 2000), 11.

14 Lisa Takats, *Red-sided Garter Snake ... Relocation and Education Project – Final Report*, Alberta SAR Report No. 30 (Edmonton: ASRD/Fish and Wildlife, 2002).

15 Map: US Fish and Wildlife Service, *Kulm Wetland Management District, North Dakota*, kulmwetlands.fws.gov/pothole.html; Ducks Unlimited Canada, *Canadian Priorities for Wetland and Wildlife Conservation Programs: Prairie-Western Boreal Region, Missouri Coteau Section* (www.ducks.ca/conserve/priorit2.html, 2005).

16 Cheryl Bradley, July 2004, *The Rumsey Wildland: Environmental Significance and Conservation History* (issues.albertawilderness.ca/RM/Archive/RP0407RM.pdf). Alberta Wilderness Association, *Rumsey* (www.albertawilderness.ca/Issues/RM/rumsey.htm, 5 February 2005), 1-2.

17 Shirley Bray, "Coal Bed Methane Comes to Rumsey," Part 1, *Wild Lands Advocate* (2004) 12(6): 1-5, and Part 2, *Wild Lands Advocate* (2005) 13(1): 4-9. Also, Renata

D'Aliesio, "Energy Firm Gets OK to Drill in Rumsey Protected Area," *Calgary Herald*, 10 March 2007: B3.

18 Dick Dekker, "Lament for a Dying Lake," *Edmonton Nature News*, Jan./Feb. 2005, map, page 9. Shawn Ohier, "Troubled Water: Beaverhill Lake near Tofield is Down to a Sixth of Its Peak Size," *Edmonton Journal*, 4 July 2006.

19 The festival was once the largest birding event in Canada, attracting about 6,000 visitors a year, according to the City of Edmonton's tourism department.

20 Conversation with authors, 14 August 2002.

21 Natural Resources Canada, *Atlas of Canada – Climate Change*, maps, text, atlas.nrcan.gc.ca/site/english/maps/climatechange.

22 Conversations with authors, 15 and 16 August 2002.

FOOTHILLS – WELLSPRING OF LIFE

1 Alberta Wilderness Association, *Bighorn Wildland* (Calgary: AWA, 2003), 16-21.

2 Richard Thomas, *Selecting Protected Areas: The Foothills Natural Region of Alberta* (Edmonton: Alberta Environmental Protection, 1996).

3 Ibid., 59, 61n.

4 Alberta Woodland Caribou Recovery Team, *Alberta Woodland Caribou Recovery Plan 2004/5 – 2013/14*, ASAR Plan No. 4 (Edmonton: ASRD/Fish and Wildlife, 2005), 21, 23-24. Hanneke Brooymans, "Alberta Killing Off Wolves to Save Hinton-area Caribou. One-sided Plan Should Also Limit Industry: Critics," *Edmonton Journal*, www.Canada.com, 11 January 2006.

5 Cutting rights: Elizabeth May, *At the Cutting Edge: The Crisis in Canada's Forests*, revised edition (Toronto: Key Porter Books, 2005), 267. International loggers: Dianne Pachal, pers. comm., 15 December 2006, and Richard R. Schneider, *Alternative Futures: Alberta's Boreal Forest at the Crossroads* (Edmonton: Federation of Alberta Naturalists and Alberta Centre for Boreal Research, 2002), 21.

6 Ibid., 278.

7 Forest Ethics, "Top Catalogs Branded as Endangered Forest Destroyers" (22 March 2004), forestethics.org/article.php?id=1283.

8 David Boyd, public lecture (Calgary, 8 January 2005).

9 Jobs: Alberta Forest Products Association, *Facts and Figures* (Edmonton: AFPA, 2006), www.albertaforestproducts.ca/industry/facts_figures.aspx. Royalties: Alberta Finance, "Fiscal Plan," *Provincial Budget* (Edmonton: www.finance.gov.ab.ca/publications/budget).

10 Dagmar Timmer, "Grandfather to a New Generation of Foresters," *World Conservation* (1999) 3(4): 25-26.

11 Formerly named the Cheviot mine.

12 Biological hotspot: David Schindler et al., "Position Statement of Scientists on the Proposed Cheviot Open-pit Coal Mine" (Edmonton: Federation of Alberta Naturalists, February 1998), www.fanweb.ca/cheviot/index_html?main_page_name=scientists_statement.htm.

13 Plants: Alberta Native Plant Council, *Whitehorse Wildland Park* (Edmonton: ANPC, 2006), www.anpc.ab.ca/content/whitehorse_wildland_park.php.

14 Sierra Legal Defence Fund et al., "Controversial Alberta Open-pit Coal Mine Project Faces Next Legal Challenge: Conservation Groups Argue Project Will Destroy Sensitive Migratory Bird Habitat;" media release and backgrounder (Vancouver: SLDF, 2 November 2004).

15 Mining Watch Canada, *Backgrounder: Cheviot Mine* (Ottawa: MWC, 13 April 2004 and 11 August 2005), www.miningwatch.ca.

BOREAL FOREST – FREEZE-DRIED ZONE

1 Libby Gunn, *Thebacha Trails: A Guide to Special Areas around Fort Smith, Northwest Territories* (Vancouver: Libby Gunn, 2000). Parks Canada's Wood Buffalo National Park web page: www.pc.gc.ca/pn-np/nt/woodbuffalo/index_E.asp.

2 Key role: Mark Hebblewhite et al., "Human Activity Mediates a Trophic Cascade Caused by Wolves," *Ecology* (January 2005) 86(8): 2135-44. Wolves: Alberta Sustainable Resource Development, *Present Status of the Wolf* (Edmonton: ASRD/FW, 27 May 2002), www.srd.gov.ab.ca/fishwildlife/wildlifeinalberta/wolvesalberta/presentstatus.aspx.

3 Tom Stehn, *Latest Whooping Crane Update* (Texas: Aransas NWR, 29 June 2006). Stehn is the U.S. Fish and Wildlife Service whooping crane coordinator. Conservation history: "Whooping Crane," Cornell Lab of Ornithology's *Bird Guide* web pages.

4 Richard Thomas, *Making Connections: Alberta's Neotropical Migratory Birds* (Calgary: Mono Congo Joint Venture, 1994).

5 Stuart Macmillan, wildlife biologist, Wood Buffalo National Park, Fort Smith, NT, pers. comm., 17 August 2006.

6 Environment Canada, *Peace-Athabasca Delta, Alberta – Ramsar Site* (Ottawa, 3 January 2007 update), www.mb.ec.gc.ca/nature/whp/ramsar/dfo2so6.en.html.

7 Muskrat and waterfowl: David Schindler, "The Effects of Climate Warming and Cumulative Human Activity on Canada's Freshwater in the 21st Century," *Water and the Future of Life on Earth*, workshop proceedings (Burnaby, BC: Simon Fraser University, 22-24 May 2002). Ed Struzik, "Alberta Natives Vow to Fight Site C," *Edmonton Journal*, 3 July 2004. Alberta Environment, "Section 3.5, Flow Regulation – Effects on the Peace-Athabasca Delta," *Northern River Basins Study Final Report*, revised (Edmonton: AE, 8 July 1996).

8 Alberta Online Encyclopedia, "The Mountain Rapids of the Slave River." www.abheritage.ca/abnature/shield/featured_slave_river.htm.

9 Senate Subcommittee on the Boreal Forest, *Competing Realities: The Boreal Forest at Risk* (Ottawa: Senate of Canada, June 1999), 10, www.parl.gc.ca/36/1/parlbus/commbus/senate/com-e/rep-e.htm.

10 Premier's speech at the Western Governors' Association North American Energy Summit in Albuquerque, New Mexico, April 2004.

11 Richard Schneider and Simon Dyer, *Death by a Thousand Cuts: Impacts of In Situ Oil Sands Development on Alberta's Boreal Forest* (Calgary: Pembina Institute/CPAWS, August 2006), vii, www.pembina.org.

12 Ibid., 19.

13 Pembina Institute, *Government Must Rein in Disorderly Development, Balance with Environmental Protection*, media release, 19 September 2006.

14 Andrew Nikiforuk, "Pine Plague," *Canadian Geographic* (January/February 2007), 68-76.

CANADIAN SHIELD – BONES OF THE EARTH

1 Gunn, *Thebacha Trails*, 46.

2 Ibid., 45.

3 Alberta Fish and Wildlife, "White Pelican: Limiting Factors," 17 June 2002, www.srd.gov.ab.ca/fishwildlife/speciesatrisk/selectedprofiles/whitepelican.aspx.

4 Gunn, *Thebacha Trails*, 50.

5 Jacques van Pelt, pers. comm., March 2005.

6 Johnnie Desjarlais in conversation with the authors, 7 September 2001.

OLD POLITICS – LOSING OUR WAY

1 E.O. Wilson, speech to State of the Planet Symposium, Earth Institute, March 2004.

2 Jeffrey Wilson and Mark Anielski, *Ecological Footprints of Canadian Municipalities and Regions* (Edmonton: Anielski Management Inc., January 2005), update

prepared for the Federation of Canadian Municipalities. David Suzuki Foundation, *The Maple Leaf in the OECD: Comparing Progress towards Sustainability* (Vancouver: DSF, 2005).

3 Darlene Howat (Alberta Environment), email, 20 March 2007, Alberta Energy's *Annual Report 2005-6*, 14, and Alberta Environment's 16 February 2007 web page, www3.gov.ab.ca/env/soe/land_indicators/40_oilgas_reclamation.html. In round numbers, industry has drilled 330,000 oil and gas wells in Alberta, of which 206,000 are active. When of no further use, the wells are legally required to be properly decommissioned ("abandoned"): rendered incapable of flow and the casing capped about a metre below ground. Then the site must be properly reclaimed (returned to a state as productive as prior to drilling) and certified by Alberta Environment as such. From 1 October 2003, reclamation also includes contamination remediation. So far, just over 51,500 of the roughly 125,000 "suspended" (disused) sites have been reclaimed.

This leaves about 73,500 disused sites unreclaimed, for 37,500 of which the corporations concerned are liable. The other nearly 36,000 are wells abandoned on private land before 1963 or on public land before 1978 – dates when reclamation became law. So their corporate owners are exempt from the law. This is huge liability.

If the corporations responsible go out of business, the wells are termed "orphaned." Liability for abandoning and reclaiming (including remediating) orphan wells (and other related facilities and pipelines) is beginning to be picked up by the industry as a whole via the Orphan Wells Association, which came into being in January 2002.

Reclamation typically costs $20,000 to $40,000 per site. But the huge backlog of older wells unreclaimed and even uncertified as abandoned is a costlier liability. One old Turner Valley well cost $0.7 million to abandon. Three historic Peace River wells cost a total of $5 million to abandon in 2003 (see Orphan Well Association annual reports, www.orphanwell.ca). The remediation and reclamation of sites over 40 years old can cost half a million dollars apiece.

Meanwhile, from 1996 to 2006, while some 3,600 wells have been abandoned annually, only 45 percent have been reclaimed. So the backlog added to the exempt wells grows worse every year.

4 Mary Griffiths et al., *Troubled Waters, Troubling Trends: Technology and Policy Options to Reduce Water Use in Oil and Oil Sands Development in Alberta – Report* (Calgary: Pembina Institute, May 2006), 72.

5 Alberta Finance, *It's Your Future*, October 2004. Top Canadian issue: Ipsos Reid polls, "An overwhelming

85 percent of Canadians are concerned about climate change," 11 June 2006 and 16 March 2007.

6 Dennis Soron, "The Politics of De-Politicization: Neo-Liberalism and Popular Consent in Alberta," in Trevor W. Harrison, ed., *The Return of the Trojan Horse* (Montreal: Black Rose Books/Institute of Policy Alternatives of Montreal, 2005).

7 Stephen Castle, "Blair Hails 'Bold' EU Deal to Slash Carbon Emissions and Boost Renewable Power," *The Independent*, London, 9 March 2007, news.independent.co.uk/europe/article2344770.ece.

8 J. Brad Stelfox, presentation to Canadian Parks and Wilderness Society annual general meeting, Calgary, September 2006.

9 Pembina Institute, *Government Spending on Canada's Oil and Gas Industry* (Calgary: PI, 2005).

10 Amy Taylor, *Genuine Progress Indicators: Summary Report Alberta* (Calgary: Pembina Institute, September 2005).

11 Boyd, *Unnatural Law*, 252.

12 Environment Canada, Canada's 2004 *Greenhouse Gas Inventory: A Summary of Trends*, www.ec.gc.ca/pdb/ghg/inventory_report/2004/2004summary_e.cfm. Canada's greenhouse emissions reached 758 megatonnes in 2004; its Kyoto target was 563 megatonnes.

13 Natural Resources Canada, *The State of Canada's Forests 2002-2003*. Alberta SRD/Public Lands and Forests, *Forests: Enforcement and Compliance – 2005 Contraventions* (Edmonton: ASRD/PLAF, 2006). Calgary Public Library staff, pers. comm., 18 January 2006.

14 Nicholas Stern, *Stern Review: The Economics of Climate Change* (Cambridge: Cambridge University Press, 2006).

15 The David Suzuki Foundation, Pembina Institute, and many others show how Canada could make huge reductions in GHG emissions. In his book, *Heat* (2006), journalist George Monbiot explains how a 90 percent reduction in Britain is possible by 2030, using existing technologies.

16 Panel on the Ecological Integrity of Canada's National Parks, *"Unimpaired for Future Generations"? Protecting Ecological Integrity with Canada's National Parks, Vol. I: A Call to Action* (Ottawa: Parks Canada, 2000), 2-6.

17 Elizabeth May, *At the Cutting Edge: The Crisis in Canada's Forests*, revised edition (Toronto: Key Porter Books, 2005), 279.

NEW LIFESTYLES – FINDING THE PATH

1 David Suzuki and Holly Dressel, *From Naked Ape to Superspecies* (Toronto: Stoddart, 1999), 255.

2 George Monbiot, "How Much Reality Can You Take?" *Guardian*, 21 September 2006, www.monbiot.com/archives/2006/09/21.

3 Harvey Locke, "Y2Y Meeting Transcript" (Canmore, AB: Y2Y, 2004).

4 Canadian Boreal Initiative, www.borealcanada.ca.

5 Northern Plains Conservation Network news release, 27 February 2004, www.npcn.net/release.htm.

6 City of Calgary, *Calgary Transit and the Environment: Ride the Wind*, www.calgarytransit.com/environment/ride_d_wind.html.

7 Drake Landing Solar Community, www.dlsc.ca. R-2000 is a Natural Resources Canada building standard for new-home energy efficiency, air quality, etc., that goes far beyond building code standards. See the Canadian Home Builders Association web site: r2000.chba.ca.

8 Alberta Agriculture and Food, 2007 *Alberta Farmers' Markets*, www.agric.gov.ab.ca/app21/rtw/markets/markets.jsp. There are more than 100 such markets across the province. Patagonia: Yvon Chouinard, *Let My People Go Surfing* (London: Penguin, 2005), 238.

9 J. Brad Stelfox, presentation to Canadian Parks and Wilderness Society AGM, Calgary, 11 September 2006.

10 Aurum Lodge, www.aurumlodge.com. See also www.audubonintl.org/programs/greenleaf/index.htm.

Measurement Conversions

1 kilometre (km)
= 0.62 miles (mi)

1 mile
= 1.6 kilometres

1 square kilometre (km^2)
= 0.4 square mile (mi^2)
= 100 hectares (ha)

1 section of land
= 1 mi^2
= 640 acres
= 2.59 km^2
= 259 ha

1 tonne (metric ton, 1,000 kg, 2,205 lb)
= 0.98 UK ton (long ton, 2,240 lb)
= 1.10 US ton (short ton, 2,000 lb)

INDEX

NR = Natural Region; SR = Subregion

Please Protect Wild Alberta